FOREVER FAITHFUL

FOREVER FAITHFUL

CELEBRATING THE GREATEST MOMENTS OF CORNELL HOCKEY

JIM ROBERTS WITH **ARTHUR MINTZ**

FOREWORD BY KEN DRYDEN

☰ THREE HILLS

AN IMPRINT OF CORNELL UNIVERSITY PRESS

ITHACA AND LONDON

First published 2017 by Cornell University Press

Printed in Canada

Design and composition by Scott Levine

Library of Congress Cataloging-in-Publication Data

Names: Roberts, Jim, 1949– author. | Mintz, Arthur, researcher. | Dryden, Ken, 1947– writer of foreword.
Title: Forever faithful : celebrating the greatest moments of Cornell hockey / Jim Roberts with Arthur Mintz ; foreword by Ken Dryden.
Description: Ithaca ; London : Three Hills, an imprint of Cornell University Press, 2017. | Includes index.
Identifiers: LCCN 2017000086 (print) | LCCN 2017002224 (ebook) | ISBN 9781501702600 (cloth : alk. paper) | ISBN 9781501712319 (ebook) | ISBN 9781501709678 (pdf)
Subjects: LCSH: Cornell University—Hockey. | Hockey—New York (State)—Ithaca—History.
Classification: LCC GV847.75.C67 R64 2017 (print) | LCC GV847.75.C67 (ebook) | DDC 796.962/630974771—dc23
LC record available at https://lccn.loc.gov/2017000086

Cornell University Press strives to use environmentally responsible suppliers and materials to the fullest extent possible in the publishing of its books. Such materials include vegetable-based, low-VOC inks and acid-free papers that are recycled, totally chlorine-free, or partly composed of nonwood fibers. For further information, visit our website at www.cornellpress.cornell.edu.

Photos in front matter:
i: Assistant captain Laura Fortino displays the 2013 ECAC championship trophy as she and her teammates enjoy the win. (Patrick Shanahan/Cornell Athletic Communications)
ii: Cornell salutes the Lynah Faithful in celebration of a victory over Harvard on home ice, March 1, 2014. (Courtesy of Ned Dykes, Cornell Hockey Association)
xi: Head coach Ned Harkness and seniors John Hughes, Dan Lodboa, Gordie Lowe, Garth Ryan, and Steve Giuliani celebrate the 1967 NCAA championship. (Jim Cunningham/Cornell Athletic Communications)

In the chapter "The Games," content for "Ned Harkness, Motivator" is from Robert J. Kane, *Good Sports: A History of Cornell Athletics* (Cornell University, 1992), used by permission.

™

CONTENTS

Ken Dryden thought that coming to Cornell would be "good preparation for law school." He was also pleased that he could play hockey, although he didn't believe he would have an opportunity to go on to play professionally. (Cornell Athletic Communications)

FOREWORD

KEN DRYDEN '69

I ARRIVED AT CORNELL IN SEPTEMBER 1965.

I was going to be a government major. I had met Clinton Rossiter, the school's famed expert on the American presidency, during a high school senior visit, and I came away from that visit thinking politics and world affairs seemed important. Studying government promised to be good preparation for law school. I also wanted to live in the United States for a time. I had grown up in a suburb of Toronto during the early years of TV, within easy range of the Buffalo stations, and I was interested in all things American. My favorite movie stars were American, my favorite singers, comedians, college football teams, and TV shows—Jackie Gleason, Ed Sullivan, *Bonanza* (which starred Lorne Greene, a Canadian), *Perry Mason* (ditto—Raymond Burr), and others. The politics I followed were Democratic and Republican more than Liberal and Conservative. Cornell would be an adventure.

I also wanted to play hockey. Lynah Rink had been built only a few years earlier, and Ned Harkness, who had won an NCAA championship at Rensselaer Polytechnic Institute, had been hired as coach. Cornell had hockey *ambitions*.

The NHL had only six teams at the time. Almost all its players, and all its stars, were Canadian. Like me, they had been developed outside schools on club teams through a grind of seventy-game seasons. This, NHL managers believed, made junior hockey–trained players better and tougher than those trained in thirty-game U.S. high school and college seasons. Also, having little time for their education, many Canadian players dropped out of school—with few other options for their future, hockey mattered to them more, or so these managers thought. At the time, NHL teams didn't need U.S. college players and didn't want them.

I understood this, but it didn't matter to me at the time because I knew I would never play in the NHL. The NHL was an impossibly distant world of players who skated too fast and shot too hard. College hockey, on the other hand, would give me a few more years of doing what I loved to do. Then I would go back to Canada, probably to a Toronto suburb like the one in which I had grown up, and practice law.

Ultimately, my future turned out—as it did for most of my fellow incoming Cornell classmates—almost nothing like what I imagined.

I loved Cornell. I loved being away and feeling on my own. I loved the *night-is-day/day-is-night, work-is-play/play-is-work* life that we lived. I loved the intensity of the times, the stakes that were ever present, always high—war, race—the academic and the real coming together. It was exciting to be on campus: the marches and the protests; the takeover of the Straight; the Joan Baez concert on April 5, 1968, the day after Martin Luther King Jr. was assassinated. I loved the possibilities of the place. I came to Cornell knowing I was a good goalie for being a good student, and a good student for being a good goalie. But because of something a few teachers and one coach saw in me, I came to realize I was both a good goalie and a good student.

I remember hockey at Cornell.

I remember my first game: freshmen versus varsity, November 1965. Freshmen at the time couldn't compete on any NCAA varsity team. Playing Junior B hockey at home, about seventy people—parents and girlfriends of those on both teams—would watch us play. That night at Cornell, when our locker-room door opened and I walked toward the ice, Lynah was jammed with four thousand screaming fans who had waited eight months to see their team again. At the end of the second period, we were winning. We lost to the varsity, but when the game was over, I thought, *Wow, I'm going to like it here.*

Then, just as quickly we turned into freshmen/pumpkins again, playing non-games against non-teams in front of twelve patient, shivering girlfriends—no parents—the rest of the year.

I remember some breakthrough moments in my sophomore year. Our third game was on the road in Potsdam against Clarkson, who had beaten Cornell in the ECAC final the year before. The rink was ancient, tiny, and frigid. A *Sports Illustrated* writer, Mark Mulvoy, had traveled with us, giving national attention to our program. We won, 3–2.

A month later we played Boston University in the final of the Boston Arena Christmas Tournament. Both squads were unbeaten, and easily the two best teams in the East. With less than five minutes remaining, BU tied the game 3–3, and we went into overtime, then double overtime. With neither team able to score, tournament officials stopped the game and named us co-champions. We would meet again, and we both knew it.

I remember the NCAA Tournament in Syracuse, watching North Dakota practice the night before we would play them in the semifinals. They looked so fast, and the West always beat the East. We won, 1–0.

Two nights later, we played BU again. We had defeated them a week earlier in the ECAC final at Boston Garden in a very close game, 4–3. I remember the warm-up. I played in a "bad-equipment era" for goalies. When we stopped shots, the puck hurt, especially when we got hit in the upper body or face. So I tried to catch almost every shot, even those in front of my chest, on my blocker side, or along the ice—because catching a shot felt good, and it didn't hurt. Then in the warm-up—a shot low to my left, my left leg pad shoots out; one high to my right, my blocker deflects it to the corner. Suddenly, I wasn't just a "kid with a good glove hand," I was a "goalie."

We won, 4–1.

I remember the losses: Against Yale at Lynah, the only defeat of our 1966–67 season. The next year at Brown, 6–3, then in the NCAA semifinals in Duluth against North Dakota. My senior year, losing at RPI and in the NCAA finals in Colorado Springs against Denver. The games against Yale, Brown, and RPI we should have won; the games against North Dakota and Denver, we might have won but didn't.

In all the eighty-three games I played, I remember only one save. It happened against Harvard late in the ECAC final my senior year. The puck was passed in front of our net, and their player shot it quickly along the ice to my stick-side corner. I threw out my skate; the puck disappeared. Not visible to one side or in front of me, it could only be in the net, and the Harvard players began celebrating. I looked down; the puck was wedged between my skate and my pad.

I remember our teams. We were good in 1968, better in 1969, but the best team I ever played on was in 1967. We had some talented sophomores like Brian Cornell, Bruce Pattison, Peter Tufford, and Bob McGuinn who would have outstanding seasons ahead. We had a junior defenseman, Skip Stanowski, who scored the winning goal against North Dakota that year in the NCAAs. But above all, we had great seniors, stars like the Ferguson twins, Doug and Dave, Mike Doran, and Harry Orr, and solid non-stars like Murray Deathe, Paul Althouse, Bob Kinasewich, and the youngest Ferguson brother, Bob—a group that was tough, dedicated, and knew how to win. That team may or may not be the greatest in Cornell history. It was not the most legendary—the unbeaten, untied 1970 team was—but it was surely the

After graduating, Dryden won six Stanley Cups in eight years with the NHL's Montreal Canadiens. He was inducted into the Hockey Hall of Fame in 1983, his first year of eligibility, and served as a member of Canada's Parliament from 2004 to 2011. (Frank Prazak/Hockey Hall of Fame, used by permission)

most important. It showed that an eastern team could win, that a nonscholarship school could win, that Cornell could win.

Maybe most of all, I remember the fans. The ones who camped out overnight in raw Ithaca weather to get their season tickets. The ones who went on the road with us, to Christmas tournaments in Boston or New York, and the two or three thousand who sounded like ten thousand at the ECACs in Boston Garden. They taught us a life lesson—always do what you do where it matters.

In 1971, two years after I graduated, I was back in Boston Garden to play for the Montreal Canadiens in the first round of the Stanley Cup playoffs against the Boston Bruins. At that time, I had played in only six NHL games; the Bruins were the defending Cup champions. I remember skating out onto the ice for the first game. The Garden was jammed; the fans screamed. The Stanley Cup playoffs are a competition like no other, I was told. I was soon immersed in the game, and while we lost, when it was over I realized something. A jammed arena, screaming fans, a championship at stake: I had been there before. Six weeks later, we were the Stanley Cup champions. When I graduated from Cornell in 1969, it turned out I was ready for much more than I knew.

FOREVER FAITHFUL

The history of Cornell hockey hangs in the Lynah Rink rafters: banners for championships and NCAA Tournament appearances by the men's and women's programs, from the 1960s to the present—and the only two numbers retired by the Big Red, Dryden 1 and Nieuwendyk 25. (Ned Dykes, Cornell Hockey Association)

PROLOGUE

LYNAH RINK doesn't look like much from the outside—a squat brick building with an arched roof, wedged between a parking lot and Bartels Hall. As you walk in, making your way down a hallway and around a corner, it could be just about any 1950s-era athletic building on any college campus. If you're a student, you head for section A or B on the south side of the ice; if you're a townie, you go to the other side, walking past the concession stand and perhaps pausing to look through a window to watch the players warming up. More doors, another hallway, and then you walk through the entrance to your section. And you look up.

There, hanging from the aged wooden rafters, are the banners. Dozens of them—red for the men's team, white for the women's team: Ivy League Champions, ECAC Champions, NCAA Tournament, NCAA Champions. Two oversize red jerseys hang over center ice: Dryden 1, Nieuwendyk 25—the only numbers retired by the Big Red program, in honor of two of the most accomplished players ever to skate on the ice of Lynah.

No matter how many games you've attended or what you may think about that year's team, that sight never loses its magic. It inspires players, coaches, and fans and intimidates opponents. Before the songs and the cheers and the shouts of "Sieve!" begin, it's seeing all the proud history represented by that array of banners that sets the scene. You're in the home of Cornell hockey, one of the greatest programs in American intercollegiate athletics and the source of pride for generations of Cornellians.

You understand what it means to be a member of the Lynah Faithful.

The feeling that comes from stepping into Lynah Rink persists, even when the Big Red teams go on the road—whether it's to Harvard (where so many Cornell fans show up for games that Bright Hockey Center has been dubbed "Lynah East"), the Herb Brooks Arena at Lake Placid, or Madison Square Garden on the Saturday night after Thanksgiving.

The Cornell fans who learned the game and the traditions at Lynah carry that atmosphere with them. They shout "Red!"

during the national anthem and "Fight!" after hearing a familiar rhythm banged out on a cowbell. They sing "Far Above Cayuga's Waters" before the third period. The Cornell hockey traditions have been widely imitated but never equaled. There may be other universities with more impressive facilities, but there's nothing like Lynah Rink. Programs like Boston College and the University of Michigan have more national championships, but the reputation of Big Red hockey stands out. Being a member of the Lynah Faithful is something that stays with you all your life.

Great hockey games linger in the memory, and just talking about them years later can inspire strong feelings. The contests described here all stand out for one reason or another—some won championships; others featured outstanding performances by individuals or entire teams. They were selected to provide an overview of different aspects of the Cornell program's history, but they are not the complete story, which is far too deep and rich for a single volume. You probably have vivid memories of other games. I hope you do.

※ ※ ※

When Lynah Rink opened, the arena's first public address announcer, Barlow Ware '47, began his pregame announcements with a simple greeting. When Arthur Mintz '71 took over the job in 1987, he continued the tradition—and to this day, every home game begins with that same greeting. No phrase triggers more emotions for Cornell hockey fans than those four words.

So let's begin this celebration of the greatest moments in Cornell hockey by saying:
"GOOD EVENING, HOCKEY FANS."

THE RINK

BEFORE THERE WAS LYNAH RINK, there was a lake—Beebe Lake, which is really just a pond. And not a very big one. It was the site of Cornell's first home hockey games, although the team had been playing for several years before they competed on campus.

There was interest in the game as far back as 1894, when an item in the *Cornell Daily Sun* noted that "a number of athletic enthusiasts are playing hockey on the ice." Two years later, the *Sun* stated: "A movement is on foot looking towards the organization of a hockey team. There are several Canadians and others in the University who are very anxious to see this sport inaugurated at Cornell." It took a few years, but the Big Red team was ready for intercollegiate competition by the turn of the century.

As former athletic director Bob Kane '34 reported in his book, *Good Sports: A History of Cornell Athletics*, Cornell's first hockey team played three games in 1900–01, all of them in Philadelphia. Coached by graduate student G. A. Smith, the squad recorded victories over Swarthmore, Penn, and Princeton. In

1907, a hockey rink was laid out on Beebe Lake under the guidance of engineering professor Johnny Parson 1899, a skating enthusiast. Practices and games were often canceled because the ice was bad—or not there at all. But on February 9, 1907, Cornell's team recorded its first home victory, a 7–0 win over the University of Rochester. A week later, they followed up with a 4–0 triumph over Army. Those were the only games that year.

Play continued, haphazardly and under various leaders, for the next nine winters. The 1910–11 team, under the guidance of Talbot Hunter, its first full-time coach, went 10–0 and won the championship of the Eastern Intercollegiate League (an early predecessor of the Ivy League). All the games were played at out-of-town arenas, presumably because the Beebe Lake conditions were unsuitable for serious competition. There were no games from 1916 to 1919 because of the First World War, but they resumed in peacetime.

In 1920, a certain degree of stability was introduced when

Beginning in 1907, Cornell played its home games on Beebe Lake. Practices and games were subject to Ithaca's unpredictable winter weather, and spectators stood on the ice behind makeshift wooden boards. (Courtesy of the Division of Rare and Manuscript Collections, Cornell University Library)

Nicky Bawlf was hired as the head coach. A former professional hockey player in Canada, he would remain in charge of the program for the next twenty-seven years. During most of Bawlf's tenure, the team played only five or six games a season. There were no games at all in the 1931–32 and 1932–33 school years, and only two in 1933–34 (a tie and a loss). A shortage of suitable opponents was one problem—and the uncertain conditions on Beebe Lake was another.

For all of its reputation as a town with tough winters, Ithaca is not Saskatoon. Today's ice often becomes tomorrow's slush. In the early days, Lou Mobbs, a groundskeeper at the universi-ty's golf course, had the job of preparing Beebe Lake for hockey games. "We would go to the lake and paint lines on the ice," he recalled in a *Cornell Alumni News* article, "and chances were it would thaw the next day. You never knew from one day to the next day if you had skating."

Dave Cutting '48, who played for Bawlf before and after the Second World War, described the playing conditions to Bob Kane: "It was primitive hockey during my time. . . . Ice on Beebe Lake was never a certainty. There were ten-inch-wide wooden sideboards around the perimeter of the rink. We piled snow closely outside to cushion the falls when we were body-check-ing along the boards. There were usually wide cracks in the ice surface. Thaws melted the ice every so often, and the boards would float away and we would have to retrieve them and nail them back together to await the next freeze."

After Bawlf's death following the 1946–47 season, the team carried on for one more year under Arthur Boeringer, an as-sistant football coach. They lost all four games by a combined score of 43–3—and that was it for Cornell hockey for the next ten years. The program was suspended.

※ ※ ※

A new era dawned in the 1957–58 school year, after Lynah Rink was constructed. Student interest in both hockey and recre-ational skating was strong, and there had been talk of build-ing a facility for years—but, as always, the question was how to fund it. The answer to that began with a conversation be-tween Walter S. Carpenter Jr. 1910, chairman of E. I. du Pont de

Nicky Bawlf (far right) coached the men's team from 1920 until 1947. In many of those years, the team played only five or six games, although his 1939–40 squad finished 5–6, capping the season with a shutout of Syracuse. (Courtesy of the Division of Rare and Manuscript Collections, Cornell University Library)

Nemours, the chemical company, and Bob Kane at a luncheon in Philadelphia before the Cornell-Penn football game in 1954.

Kane tells the story in *Good Sports*, and it begins with Carpenter approaching him and expressing interest in making a substantial gift for building an indoor rink. After he returned to Ithaca, Kane reported the conversation to President Deane Malott. Two weeks later, Malott confirmed that Carpenter intended to give the money. Alas, shortly after that Malott told Kane that Carpenter had changed his mind and was instead going to fund an engineering library, which became Carpenter Hall. Naturally, Kane was disappointed—but he conceded that "there's no doubt an engineering library is more important to the

The funds for building Lynah Rink were provided by Walter Carpenter, who requested that the new facility be named for his friend James Lynah (pictured at left as a Cornell student and at right in 1933), who had been Cornell's athletic director from 1935 to 1943. (Courtesy of the Division of Rare and Manuscript Collections, Cornell University Library)

The first game at Lynah Rink was an exhibition between the NHL's New York Rangers and the AHL's Rochester Americans on March 21, 1957, before a full house of more than four thousand spectators. (Courtesy of the Division of Rare and Manuscript Collections, Cornell University Library)

university than a hockey rink."

That seemed to be the end of it. But then Carpenter—perhaps encouraged by Malott—offered an additional gift of $500,000 from his foundation to build a rink. The only condition was that it be named for someone else; he thought that one campus building with his name on it was sufficient. Kane suggested naming it for James D. Lynah 1905, who had worked for DuPont as a plant manager before serving as Cornell's athletic director from 1935 to 1943. "The president approved," wrote Kane, "and [he] called Carpenter, who was highly pleased"—and thus spared thousands of future hockey fans from being called the Carpenter Faithful.

The architecture firm Von Storch, Evans, and Burkavage of Waverly, Pennsylvania, designed the building, and Streeter Associates of Elmira, New York, was the general contractor. Ground was broken on June 5, 1956, and work was completed the following spring.

The first game at Lynah Rink was an exhibition between the National Hockey League's New York Rangers and the American Hockey League's Rochester Americans on March 21, 1957, that drew 4,116 spectators. A *Cornell Daily Sun* editorial that day expressed enthusiasm for the facility: "The new rink represents a welcome triumph of man over nature. After struggling with an unpredictable Beebe, winter after winter, the Athletic Association finally was blessed with funds for an indoor skating rink. And this means that not only will Cornell have an official hockey team within a few years, but also that both students and area residents will have much-desired skating facilities."

At the building's dedication sixteen days later, President

Malott presented a scroll to James Lynah's widow, Elizabeth Beckwith Lynah 1903, that stated: "Cornell University dedicates to the memory of James Lynah the James Lynah Hall, to be used by the Cornell community for healthful sport and in good fellowship."

The Cornell hockey program was back, and the first varsity team of the Lynah era took the ice that fall.

✤ ✤ ✤

Lynah Rink was a state-of-the-art facility for its time, a sturdy brick structure with a 200' x 85' ice surface surrounded by wooden-bench seating on three sides. At first, seating capacity was vague, as there were no numbers on the benches and spectators would just squeeze closer together (or sit in the aisles). The fire marshal eventually frowned on that, and official capacity was set at 3,826. Wire netting provided some protection to fans sitting behind the goals, and a large scoreboard was mounted on the west wall. There was a small office for the hockey coach and a dressing room for the team—the men's team, that is, as there would not be a women's team until more than a decade later.

In the 1960s, the wire mesh above the boards was replaced by safety glass. In the '70s, the lighting was upgraded, and twenty years later the building got a new roof. Even with those improvements, Lynah Rink maintained its rugged, barnlike character. And that's a very good thing. "What other college rink is so storied, so haunted, so idiosyncratic, so detested by visiting teams and embraced by the home team, as is Lynah?" wrote

Construction of Lynah Rink began in June 1956 and was completed the following spring. A state-of-the-art facility for its time, it was hailed in the *Cornell Daily Sun* as a "welcome triumph of man over nature." (Courtesy of the Division of Rare and Manuscript Collections, Cornell University Library)

The success of the Cornell teams of the 1960s and '70s packed Lynah Rink with spectators for every game and made it an unpleasant venue for opponents. From 1967 to 1972, the Big Red won sixty-three straight home games. (Jim Cunningham '71/Cornell Athletic Communications)

The many red and white banners hanging from the rafters in Lynah Rink celebrate the championships and NCAA Tournament appearances of both the men's and women's teams. (Courtesy of Adriano Manocchia)

In February 2010, the numbers worn by Ken Dryden and Joe Nieuwendyk were retired by the Cornell hockey program. Both of the former Big Red standouts were in attendance to see their numbers raised to the rafters. (Darl Zehr Photography/Cornell Athletic Communications)

Brad Herzog '90 in the *Cornell Alumni News* in 1993. Indeed.

In the summer of 2000, the university spent almost $1 million to pour a new rink floor, improve the refrigeration system, and install new boards and seamless glass. Seven years later, as Lynah reached its fiftieth anniversary, a $7.3 million renovation made major changes, adding some 20,000 square feet to the building. Seating capacity was increased to 4,267 by adding three rows of student-seating benches, two rows of red "luxury seats" on the townie side, and fifty-six seats on a new platform at the west end. The Big Red's bench was moved across the ice and connected to a tunnel coming from the locker rooms. A wing was added, with new locker rooms for both the men's and women's teams, coaches' lounges, study lounges, video rooms, and a training room looking out on Campus Road. Concourses were added to the north and south sides to improve fan access and provide display space for trophy cases and photographs celebrating Cornell's hockey history. Walls and doors were painted with larger-than-life images of Big Red players in action.

The players and coaches expressed gratitude for their expanded and improved facilities, but—more important—the character of the building was retained. For fans packed together on the benches and watching the action on the ice, little had changed. To this day, Lynah is cramped, cold, primitive, and hopelessly anachronistic. There is no video display hanging over center ice. The sound system doesn't blast the latest pop hits. The concession stands sell popcorn and hot coffee, not gourmet food. The place is still detested by opponents and loved by the home team. For the Big Red players and the Lynah Faithful, as Ned Harkness once put it, "there's no better place to be."

THE FANS

AS INTEREST IN CORNELL HOCKEY GREW during the 1960s, more and more spectators crowded into Lynah Rink. At first, their cheering was enthusiastic but disorganized. There was the usual encouragement of Cornell players and abuse of opponents (and officials). A few especially vociferous regulars were noted for their efforts, but that was mostly because of volume rather than originality.

Over time, certain cheers and rituals began to appear regularly, and in the ensuing years the Lynah Faithful have developed one of the most complex—and imitated—traditions in any college sport at any venue. While most of this first appeared at men's games, many of the cheers and rituals have now been adopted by the fans at women's games.

Although opponents think of Lynah as a "tough place to play," recalling the taunts sent in their direction by the Faithful, many of the cheers are positive, intended to encourage and inspire the home team. The strongest and simplest of these, yelled repeatedly when the Big Red is struggling to control the puck or an opponent has just scored, is "Let's Go Red!" (*never* "Go Big Red!"), accompanied by rhythmic clapping.

Perhaps the most venerable of the organized cheers is "We want more!"—which is shouted after the crowd counts the number of goals scored. This was an especially long cheer during such Ned Harkness–era games as the 19–0 crushing of Hamilton College on January 13, 1965, and the 15–0 obliteration of Canada's York University on November 25, 1965. And then there's the famed cowbell cheer, originated by Neil Cohen '72 during the 1968–69 season. It has been passed down to a succession of "cowbell guys" since, occasionally augmented by other instruments. "I remember hearing that cowbell," says Pete Tufford '69, an All-American forward in his senior year. "Now, they might do it only once in a game, but back then it went on throughout the game."

When the Big Red scores, Arthur Mintz announces the scoring player's name and is loudly echoed by the crowd, as in, "Cornell goal scored by number 15, Colin Greening." "GREENING!"

As interest in Cornell hockey grew during the '60s, fans filled the stands in Lynah Rink to cheer on the Big Red—and the rituals of the Lynah Faithful began to be established. (Courtesy of the Division of Rare and Manuscript Collections, Cornell University Library)

After a Big Red score, the Lynah Faithful rise to their feet, count off the Cornell goals, and announce, "We want more!" (Photo Services/Cornell Athletic Communications)

In the '60s, a skating bear mascot took to the ice between periods, helping to encourage the high spirits of the Lynah Faithful. (Courtesy of Sol Goldberg/ Division of Rare and Manuscript Collections, Cornell University Library)

As the names of the opposing players are announced, the Faithful hold up copies of the *Daily Sun* and chant "Boring!" (Photo Services/Cornell Athletic Communications)

Since 1968, a designated "cowbell guy" has been a fixture at all home games, leading raucous cheers to inspire the Big Red players. (Photo Services/Cornell Athletic Communications)

After the opponent introductions have ended, the newspapers are crumpled and thrown to the ice, where they are quickly removed by the Lynah Rink staff. (Courtesy of Adriano Manocchia)

Dave Nulle began grooming the ice between periods in the '80s. He wore a hat one night, then began to expand his wardrobe. One of his first costumes was a tuxedo—for a Harvard game. He has added many more outfits since then. (Courtesy of Ned Dykes, Cornell Hockey Association)

Multiple goals can get a special salute. Topher Scott '08 recalls his first exhibition game at Lynah, as a freshman forward: "I scored two goals, and at the end of the game the fans started chanting my name. I thought, *It doesn't get any better than this!*" Spectacular saves by a Cornell goaltender are honored by deep bows, with arms upraised, as well as the chanting of the goalie's name.

As each period nears its end, Mintz announces, "One minute remaining in the period," and the Faithful respond with a polite "Thank you!" After the players have departed for the dressing room, the ice is groomed by a Zamboni, driven by Dave Nulle. (Currently, it's an Olympia ice resurfacer, but no one calls it that.) Nulle started out at Lynah as "a guy who moves the nets around" and began to drive the Zamboni in the 1980s—usually while wearing an outlandish costume. That tradition, he explained to *Cornell Alumni Magazine* in 2009, began with a hat—"a sort of Russian babushka." He moved on to a tuxedo (for a Harvard game, of course) and eventually gathered a large collection of vintage coats, hats, capes, boots, and assorted props. He sometimes holds up a sign. Nulle's colorful outfits are always saluted by the cheers of the Faithful, and he will wave and tip his hat in response.

During the intermission, Mintz announces the scores of other games. If Harvard is losing, the Faithful will cheer. On the ice, there may be contests, mini-games featuring youth-league players, or skating bears. While the custom of having one or two students dressed in bear costumes and performing for the crowd has faded away at men's games in recent years, it's been maintained for the women by the Tompkins Girls Hockey Association's Cub Club. This organization, founded in 1995 by former Big Red player (and children's book author) Megan Shull '91, pairs young hockey players with "big sisters" on the Cornell team. They participate in off-ice activities and get together before and after games, and "little sisters" can sign up to skate in bear costumes at home games.

* * *

All of the positive energy directed at the Big Red is, of course, matched by the Faithful's equally enthusiastic abuse of the visiting team. As the opposing players are introduced, the students in sections A and B hold copies of the *Daily Sun* in front of their faces, shake them, and shout "Boring!" When Mintz says, "And now, the starting lineup for the Big Red of Cornell," they crumple the newspapers and throw them on the ice. Rink attendants hustle out and gather them up. The most important variant on this ritual is, of course, the tossing of fish to greet the visiting Harvard players (more on that later). Less spectacular, and less fragrant, is the flinging of empty—one hopes—toothpaste boxes to greet Colgate skaters.

When the game gets under way, the first anti-opponent cheer is usually "Screw BU!" This traces its origin to the heated rivalry with Boston University in the 1960s and '70s, when inventive Cornellians answered the Terrier fans who shouted "Go BU!" with "Screw BU!" and then found a way to use it against any foe by yelling "Screw BU! And [opposing school] too!"

The opposing goalie is subjected to ongoing ridicule, informed early and often that he or she is a "Sieve!" and then told,

Members of the Tompkins Girls Hockey Association's Cub Club sit behind the Cornell bench to cheer for their "big sisters" on the women's team. (Photo Services/Cornell Athletic Communications)

Even the most reserved members of the Lynah Faithful can be inspired to intimidate the opposition, whether it's with cheers, chants, flying fish—or hand-lettered signs. (Photo Services/Cornell Athletic Communications)

"You're not a sieve, you're a funnel. You're not a funnel, you're a vacuum. You're not a vacuum, you're a black hole. You're not a black hole, *you just suck!*" When the visiting netminder gives up a goal, there's a reminder that "It's all your fault!"

During stoppages in play, if opposing goalies skate back and forth along the goal line, they get the "remote control" treatment. The Faithful do a little coaching, telling them to "skate, skate, skate" and "tu-u-u-rn." As they return to the crease, they're instructed to "bend over." Some goalies will resist this, and the "bend over" chant has been known to go on for several minutes. This is just what the Faithful want—the more the opposing players listen to them, the better. The supreme example of this occurred in a men's game against Dartmouth in 1999, when Big Green goalie Nick Boucher got into it with the student section, not noticing that Cornell's David Adler '00 had gained possession of the puck at the red line. As Boucher skated over to the glass to express his opinion of section B, Adler scored into the open net.

Opposing skaters who catch an edge and take a tumble are instructed to "learn to skate!" When they commit a penalty, they are welcomed to the box with "Ahhh! See ya, you goon!" (There was a time when a certain expletive was used rather than "goon," but profanity is officially discouraged at Lynah.)

The opposing institution is often insulted directly. A designated shouter will yell the name of the school, and the students will answer, "Sucks!" (This all-purpose insult is also bellowed after Mintz announces the name of an opposing player who scores a goal.) After three repetitions of this, it's capped with a fervent "Let's Go Red!" Any school will be mocked as a "safety school," even Harvard or Yale, and the Princeton team is usually reminded that their university is in New Jersey. If the opponent has dared to bring along fans (or, worse, a band), as soon they start to make noise the students will point to their designated seating area and try to drown them out with "Section O sucks!"

The officials are not immune to the scorn of the Faithful. Ones who are deemed not up to snuff are told, "I'm blind, I'm deaf, I wanna be a ref!" They are also greeted with loud boos as they skate onto the ice before the second and third periods. This provides a useful gauge of the Faithful's opinion of the quality of the officiating: the louder the boos, the worse it is. Each year, there are usually one or two ECAC referees who are booed when introduced before the game, which is a testament to the long memories of the Faithful.

※ ※ ※

Throughout the game, the cheering is bolstered by musical support. At Lynah, this isn't done with tinny recordings blasted through the sound system, as it is at many other college rinks. The music comes from the pep band, a student-run organization, which fills the top rows of section A at every game. Before the puck is dropped, they help set the mood by welcoming the Cornell players onto the ice with an enthusiastic rendition of "Give My Regards to Davy," the university's fight song. Then, as the townies rise to their feet—the students are already standing, and will continue to do so throughout the game—they play two national anthems. First, it's "O Canada"—and as an observer

The costume may have been updated over the years, but skating bears can still be seen on the ice at Lynah Rink. (Courtesy of Adriano Manocchia)

During the third period, the pep band's tubas gather in the aisle behind the opposition bench to lead the "Die . . . drop dead . . . go home!" cheer. (Courtesy of Adriano Manocchia)

once commented, "Most of the Big Red team knows the words." "The Star-Spangled Banner" is next, and the Faithful always make sure it's ". . . the rockets' RED glare," punching their right hands in the air. (And when visiting Union fans emphasize ". . . can U see" or Clarkson fans shout ". . . through the NIGHT" to support their Golden Knights, the Faithful reply with "Suck!")

When the opponent is Harvard, the pep band always offers its rendition of the theme from *Love Story*—even if few recent students have seen that classic movie, which features a Cornell–Harvard hockey game. (Cornell wins. Ned Harkness insisted on it, as a condition of using Cornell jerseys in the filming.) When a penalty is called against an opposing player, the musicians play the menacing theme from the old TV show *Dragnet*—*dum-da-dum-dum*—to remind the visitors that their team is now in trouble.

Between the second and third periods, the pep band plays two verses of the Cornell alma mater, "Far Above Cayuga's Waters," as the students stand, arms interlocked, singing the words and swaying back and forth to the music. At the last home game, this is extended to include all six verses, with the lyrics distributed on handouts. (This is a useful reminder of why Cornellians usually sing only the first two verses.)

Just before the third period, a stirring tune welcomes the Big Red back to the ice. For years, it was "Gonna Fly Now" (aka "Theme from *Rocky*"), but more recently it's been the piece known as "Gary Glitter" (the song's actual title is "Rock and Roll, Part Two"). It concludes with the Faithful shouting, "Hey, you suck! Hey, you suck! Hey, you suck! We're going to beat the hell out of you! Rough 'em up! Rough 'em up! Go CU!"

The Cornell players love the energy this creates in the building. "When we come out for the third and they're playing that Gary Glitter song," says Topher Scott, "that's something that gets everybody jacked up to play." Women's team goalie Amanda Mazzotta '12 concurs: "My personal favorite was that song to start the third period. I'd usually sway back and forth in my crease [to the beat]."

Midway through the final period, the pep band's tuba section finds its way to the aisle behind the opposing team's bench to play "Swanee River," punctuated by shouts of "Hey [opponent]!" "Die!" "Drop dead!" and "Go home!"

The end of the game has its own set of rituals. If Cornell has a lead, the students (still standing) will yell, "Townies up!" to get everyone on their feet for the final minutes. If the Big Red is way ahead, the Faithful get out their car keys, rattle them, and yell, "Go start the bus!" (When Cornell played Army, this would be "Go start the tank!") The end of a victory is marked by the designation of Cornell as the "Winning team!" and their vanquished foe as the "Losing team!" This is usually repeated several times, as the students point to each team and cheer. If it's a Saturday night and Cornell has defeated two ECAC foes, the Faithful announce that it was a "Four-point weekend!" Win or lose, after the opposing team has left the ice, the Cornell players gather at center ice and raise their sticks to salute the Faithful.

As the crowd files out after a victory the pep band salutes Mike Schafer, the head coach of the men's team (from 1995 to

In a tradition introduced by Mike Schafer when he became the head coach, at the end of each game the Cornell players gather at center ice and raise their sticks to salute the Lynah Faithful. (Courtesy of Adriano Manocchia)

At the end of the ceremonies on Senior Night, the players join with their family members and the Lynah Faithful to sing the Cornell alma mater. (© Mark H. Anbinder, used by permission)

the present) with its version of the old Schaefer Beer theme song and the students sing: "Schafer is the one coach to have / When your hockey team's just won / Schafer's pleasure doesn't fade / Even when the game is done."

The final regular-season home game is Senior Night, and there are repeated cheers of "Thank you, seniors." After the game, the spectators remain. The lights are dimmed. Each graduating player is announced and skates around the ice in a spotlight to salute the crowd as his or her accomplishments are read aloud by Mintz. Parents and significant others then join the players on the ice. After each has been honored, they are joined by their teammates for a final salute between the Big Red players and the Lynah Faithful—a reminder of a shared legacy that is treasured on both sides of the boards.

The pep band is an integral part of the Cornell hockey experience at Lynah, and the band frequently follows the team on the road. (Courtesy of Ned Dykes, Cornell Hockey Association)

THE RIVALRIES

THESE DAYS, IF YOU ASK a member of the Lynah Faithful to name the Big Red's most important rival, the answer will be "Harvard." That's understandable—the two teams have played many memorable games, often with a championship on the line. But in the 1960s and '70s, there might have been a different response. In those days, it seemed that whenever an ECAC or tournament title was on the line, the opponent wore the scarlet and white of Boston University.

Ken Dryden wrote about the importance of BU in his celebrated memoir, *The Game*: "Our closest Eastern rival, they were the necessary other side in many of my most fundamental moments, the inspiration and competitive prod for them, irrevocably and fondly associated with them."

Cornell first faced BU in 1925, in a game played on Beebe Lake; the Terriers won, 7–2. They met again a year later (another BU victory), but that was the last time until 1965, after Ned Harkness had come to East Hill. "They were as good as there was," said Harkness in 2007, reflecting on the intensity of the competition. "They were always well schooled, and their coach, Jack Kelley, was the best coach that we played against."

Jack Parker, who later served as BU's head coach for forty years, was introduced to the Big Red as a center for the Terriers in 1966. "When I was a sophomore, Cornell was not a brand-name college hockey team," he says. "Ned Harkness had just arrived, after being very successful at RPI." Perhaps because they had taken Cornell too lightly, Parker's BU team was shocked to lose badly to the Big Red, 8–1, in that year's ECAC Tournament.

The following season, the teams met in the final of the Boston Arena Christmas Tournament in a game that was called after two overtimes, with Cornell and BU named co-champions. "Everybody would have liked to just keep playing until we got a winner," says Parker. "It shouldn't have been a tie, because it was the championship game. In any event, it was a famous game, and that kind of established the rivalry."

At the end of the 1966–67 season, Cornell and BU advanced to the ECAC championship game in Boston Garden. "I believe

In the '60s and '70s, Cornell's most important rival was Boston University. The two teams battled almost every year for the ECAC championship and met in the 1967 NCAA championship game, when this photo was taken. The Cornell players are Bob Ferguson (5) and Bob Kinasewich (14). The two rivals would meet again in the 1972 NCAA championship game. (© *Cornell Daily Sun*, used by permission /Division of Rare and Manuscript Collections, Cornell University Library)

In 1979, the Big Red defeated a Boston University team with future "Miracle on Ice" Olympic hero Jim Craig in goal. (Photo Services/Cornell Athletic Communications)

Boston University's Jack Parker faced Cornell as a player in the '60s and went on to coach the Terriers for forty years. He was behind the BU bench at the first Red Hot Hockey game in Madison Square Garden in 2007. (Courtesy of Boston University Department of Athletics)

we outshot Cornell 20 to 4 in the first period," says Parker. (The official scoresheet says it was 13 to 7.) "Dryden put on quite a show. Whenever anybody asks me, Who was the best college hockey player you ever saw? Oh, that's easy: Ken Dryden." Cornell won the game 4–3. As the two top teams in the East that year, Cornell and BU were invited to the NCAA Tournament in Syracuse; they met once again for the national championship (see "The Games").

The rivalry remained intense after Harkness departed. Dick Bertrand, his successor, had been a tri-captain of the undefeated 1970 team; during his twelve years as Cornell's head coach, his teams faced BU eighteen times, winning half the games. "BU was our stiffest rival," says Bertrand. "You want to win the league? You've got to beat BU. Harvard wasn't as big back then, probably because we beat them pretty regularly. But the games against BU were always tough."

In 1972, Cornell and BU again played for the ECAC title—but this time the Terriers won, 4–1. Both teams were selected for the NCAA Tournament, where they won their semifinal contests and faced each other again for the national championship. BU prevailed 4–0. The rivalry was at its peak. "When I was playing and when I first started coaching [in 1970], BU had two rivals," says Parker. "It was Boston College and Cornell. Everybody else paled in comparison."

In 1983, BU and five other New England teams left the ECAC to form a new conference, Hockey East, and the Cornell-BU rivalry began to fade. There were games in 2001 and 2002, when they played twice each year. (In 2001, they split two games in Boston; the next year, the Big Red swept the Terriers at Lynah.) But there were no more after that until November 2007, when Cornell faced BU at Madison Square Garden in the first Red Hot Hockey game (see "The Games").

✳ ✳ ✳

As the BU rivalry cooled, the one with Harvard heated up. In the early days of the Lynah era, when Cornell was slowly building a competitive team, Harvard was one of the best teams in the East. The Crimson's games with the Big Red were one-sided for several years, with Harvard winning by 18–0 and 13–0 in 1958–59, Cornell's first year of Ivy League competition. The domination continued for several years, with Harvard winning seven times in row—until they came to Lynah Rink on February 3, 1962 (see "The Games").

Under Ned Harkness and Dick Bertrand, the tables were turned and Cornell won most of the games with the Crimson. The rivalry got more intense in January 1973 because of a chicken. In a game at Watson Rink in Cambridge, Cornell goalie Dave Elenbaas '73 was greeted by a chicken that was tossed over the boards toward him. Some accounts say it was a dead chicken—but that's not right. "I don't know where they got that it was dead," says Elenbaas. "It was definitely a live chicken." If the Crimson fans thought their insult to the Ag school would unnerve the Future Farmers of Canada, it didn't work. Cornell won the game 5–2.

When Harvard visited Lynah the following month, a live chicken was tied to one of their goalposts (and removed by a rink worker). Cornell won that game, too. The tradition persisted,

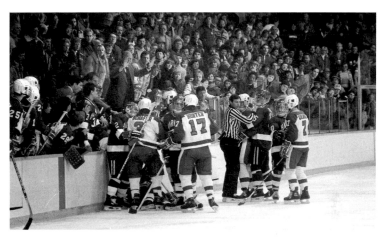

In 1983, Boston University left the ECAC to join Hockey East, and Harvard became the Big Red's number 1 rival. The competition was often intense. In this 1986 game, Cornell players exchanged opinions with legendary Crimson coach Bill Cleary. (Cornell Athletic Communications)

In 2007, when Cornell and Boston University renewed their rivalry at "The World's Most Famous Arena," the skating mascots were on hand for the festivities. (Cornell Athletic Communications)

In 1973, Harvard fans greeted the visiting Cornell players with a chicken. When the Crimson came to Lynah, the Faithful returned the favor by placing a chicken in the Harvard goal. (Tim McKinney, Cornell Athletic Communications)

and the Lynah Faithful soon began to extend the insult beyond fowl by tossing dead fish at the Harvard players, perhaps because of their school's proximity to the ocean. Or because they smell bad.

"The fish?" asked a writer in the *Harvard Crimson*, lamenting a 1981 Cornell victory. "Oh, they're just part of an age-old tradition of unstable behavior by the Ithaca masses. This year's festivities were no different from any other—the live chicken tied to the goalpost between periods, the effigies, the chants, the sieves, and finally, as the Crimson took the ice to begin the final period, the combined output of Lake Cayuga and ponds beyond flying out of the stands, aimed at the hated Crimson jerseys. Pretty funny. When the piscine onslaught continued during play, referee Pierre Belanger took measures to control the crowd, punishing the Big Red with a two-minute minor for delay of game."

A case could be made for a rivalry with Clarkson—the two teams have met repeatedly in the ECAC playoffs—but the one with Harvard remains supreme. When the Crimson come to Lynah, it's always a special event with an SRO crowd, and when the Big Red travel to Cambridge, Cornell fans crowd into "Lynah East."

✧ ✧ ✧

The same holds true for the women's team. "Harvard is such a great rivalry," says goalie Lauren Slebodnick '14. "Everyone always plays their best game." The teams first met in the 1982 Ivy League Tournament, with the Crimson winning 4–3 in

The chicken soon became a symbol of the rivalry with Harvard—and a student in a fowl costume joined the Big Red bear on the ice. (Jon Crispin, Cornell Athletic Communications)

The Cornell women's team also has a lasting rivalry with Harvard. They first met in the 1982 Ivy League Tournament, and since then they have often faced each other with an Ivy League or ECAC championship on the line. (Tim McKinney, Cornell Athletic Communications)

Dead fish eventually replaced the live chicken as a greeting for the Harvard players. Although officially discouraged, the tradition of tossing fish on the ice to welcome the Crimson to Lynah Rink lives on. (Courtesy of Adriano Manocchia)

Another key rivalry for the women has developed with Mercyhurst University. In this shot from a 2010 playoff game, Catherine White is scoring in overtime against the Lakers to send Cornell to the NCAA championship game. (Jim Rosvold/Cornell Athletic Communications)

Battles between Cornell and Harvard have often determined the ECAC Tournament championship. As of 2017, Cornell had won the Whitelaw Cup twelve times and Harvard had captured the trophy ten times. (Tim McKinney, Cornell Athletic Communications)

overtime. They have played more than eighty games since then, and between them the red-clad rivals hold the majority of Ivy League championships and ten ECAC titles.

The rivalry is enhanced by many of the familiar cheers and taunts directed at the Crimson men by the Faithful—and there was an attempt to take it further. "My senior year, we tried to incorporate one of the men's traditions: throwing fish on the ice against Harvard," says Slebodnick. "The players and fans were excited about it, but the school shut it down, threatening that anyone who brought a fish to the rink would be kicked out of the game." (It should be noted that this is official policy for the men's games against Harvard, too, but somehow the fish always find their way in.)

Head coach Doug Derraugh '91 agrees, citing Harvard as a key opponent in many important games. "Colgate is a big rival, too, because they're close by and also in our league," he says. "And Syracuse, being in the vicinity, is becoming a crosstown rival."

Another rivalry for the women's team has developed against Mercyhurst University, a small liberal arts school in Erie, Pennsylvania. The two teams first met in the 2001–02 season and have played regularly since then, often in the NCAA playoffs. "They've won some, we've won some," says Derraugh. "It's been back and forth."

Perhaps their most memorable contest was an NCAA semifinal in 2010. Mercyhurst was ranked number 1 at the time and had defeated Cornell twice at the beginning of the regular season. At the Frozen Four banquet, the Mercyhurst players exuded confidence—maybe too much. "I couldn't get over how cocky they were," recalls Catherine White '12. "Their demeanor was such that they knew they were going to win this thing. They

A series of tight regular-season and playoff games has intensified a rivalry with Boston University for the women. Their most memorable contest was a three-overtime NCAA playoff contest in 2012, the longest game ever played at Lynah Rink. (Cornell Athletic Communications)

definitely underestimated us. They acted like they were already in the final—that's what their body language was saying. We were not supposed to win that game." But they did, with White scoring a dramatic overtime goal to send the Big Red women on to the national championship game (see "The Games").

Another rivalry has developed with . . . Boston University. The teams first played in the 1982–83 season (a 2–2 tie), but did not meet again until the Frozen Four in 2011, with the Terriers coming out on top, 4–1. The rivalry was cemented the following year in the famous three-overtime playoff game at Lynah (see "The Games"), and the teams have played a series of close contests in the ensuing seasons. As it was with the men in the 1960s and '70s, the women enjoy the "inspiration and competitive prod," as Ken Dryden put it, provided by their skilled and well-coached rival from Commonwealth Avenue in Boston.

In a home game against Harvard on February 14, 1997, Kyle Knopp broke through the Crimson defense to score the first goal in a 2–1 Cornell victory. (Photo Services/ Cornell Athletic Communications)

THE GAMES

CORNELL 2, HARVARD 1
LYNAH RINK, ITHACA, NEW YORK, FEBRUARY 3, 1962

The early years in Lynah were rough and attendance was often low. Only 1,600 fans were on hand for the team's first game, a 16–3 win over a shorthanded Lehigh club team on December 14, 1957. Despite the diligent efforts of head coach Paul Patten, a string of losses followed, and the Big Red won only seven games out of fifty-three in its first three years.

The fortunes of Cornell hockey began to turn when Patten recruited three young Canadians who became the core of the 1959–60 freshman team. Forward Steve Kijanka '63, defenseman Rudy Mateka '63, and goaltender Laing Kennedy '63 were outstanding players for their junior teams in the Ontario Hockey

Association. These club teams were the primary player-development squads of their day, and most players who aspired to become professionals played several years of junior hockey rather than going to college. But Patten went north to meet these three young players and convinced them to come to Cornell.

"I was a farm boy," says Kennedy, "and I had applied to go to Ontario Agricultural College in Guelph. Coach Patten said, 'Cornell has the finest college of agriculture in the world—and I need a goalie. I think you'd fit in very well.' He gave me some brochures, and I took them home and talked to my parents. I asked my high school science teacher about Cornell, and he said, 'Laing, if you have a chance to go to Cornell and study agriculture, let me pack your bags.' That was all I needed."

The three Canadians joined a group of U.S. players, most of them from eastern prep schools, and they quickly coalesced into a strong unit. The Big Red freshmen downed the Colgate

(*facing page*) The first of many outstanding Cornell goaltenders, Laing Kennedy was recruited from Canada by Coach Paul Patten. In this landmark victory over Harvard, he made forty-eight saves. Kennedy would later serve as Cornell's athletic director from 1983 to 1994. (Courtesy of Sol Goldberg/the Division of Rare and Manuscript Collections, Cornell University Library)

Cornell hired Paul Patten as an assistant football coach in 1956. He had played football at Notre Dame before coaching both football and hockey at St. Lawrence University. In 1957, he was named head coach of the first Big Red hockey team to play in Lynah Rink. (Cornell Athletic Association)

freshmen 5–0 in their first game and went on to win eleven more, finishing the season undefeated. The varsity, meanwhile, struggled through a 2–19 campaign, losing by such scores as 13–0 to Yale and 12–2 to Harvard.

With the three Canadians on the team, the 1960–61 varsity improved to 7–12. "When we became upperclassmen, we formed and molded a team around a coach," says Mateka. Patten had been a football player in college, and he welcomed input from his players. "Coach Patten would listen to things that we suggested. We would say things like we should do *this* instead of *that*, or how about changing the lines? He would listen, because he knew that he didn't know everything about hockey. We became a real team."

The 1961–62 season began with Cornell victories in five of the first seven games, and interest in the team began to grow. "We defeated Yale and Dartmouth, and we suddenly found ourselves in second place in the Ivy League," recalls Kennedy. "We started building a fan base, and we were getting a lot of press. Leading up to that Harvard game at Lynah, you could sense that the community was really going to turn out. You just had that feeling."

At the time, most of the top college hockey programs were in the Midwest—Michigan had already won six national titles—but a few eastern schools had strong programs, including Harvard. The Crimson had won six of the last eight Ivy League championships and defeated Cornell seven times in a row, including a 5–1 drubbing at Cambridge less than a month before. Their head coach, Cooney Weiland, was considered the dean of eastern hockey coaches. He surely expected another easy win.

Lynah Rink was filled to capacity (and beyond) for the game against a Harvard team that had defeated the Big Red seven times in a row. The fans' boisterous support inspired the Cornell players that night, setting the stage for the Lynah Faithful to come. (Courtesy of Sol Goldberg/Division of Rare and Manuscript Collections, Cornell University Library)

The game featured intense end-to-end action right from the start, with the Cornell players playing "out of their skulls" and holding their own against a Crimson team that had been a dominant power in eastern hockey for years. (Courtesy of Sol Goldberg/Division of Rare and Manuscript Collections, Cornell University Library)

Despite the growing interest in Cornell's up-and-coming team, even the players were astounded as they watched Lynah Rink fill up on the night of February 3, 1962. There was general admission in those days, so the fans just kept squeezing together on the wooden benches. And then they sat in the aisles and packed all the standing-room areas. Most game accounts estimate the attendance at 4,200 to 4,500—well above what would later become the official capacity. "I would say this was the first real experience of the Lynah Faithful," says Kennedy, who served as Cornell's athletic director from 1983 to 1994. "It was

boisterous and enthusiastic. The energy was tremendous."

Cornell got an early break when Harvard's outstanding goaltender, Bob Bland, was injured in practice on the day before the game, sustaining a cut above his eye that required seven stitches. In those days goalies didn't wear masks, so it ruled him out for the game. Godfrey Wood took his place in the net. "Coach Patten says, 'OK, they're using their backup goalie,'" recalls Kennedy. "'We can score on this team.'"

The Cornell players channeled the energy of the crowd into a tremendous effort on the ice. They came out flying—and their

The 1961–62 Cornell team was anchored by three talented Canadians: Laing Kennedy (third from left, front row), Steve Kijanka (far left, front row), and Rudy Mateka (behind Kijanka, next to Coach Paul Patten). "We were inseparable," says Kennedy. (Cornell Athletic Communications)

Forward Jerry Kostandoff scored the first goal of the game, deflecting a pass from linemate Jim Stevens into the Crimson goal to put the Big Red ahead 1–0 in the second period, as the crowd roared its approval. (Cornell Athletic Communications)

Rudy Mateka anchored the defense. He says that the Harvard players may have been overconfident—"they'd been beating the pants off us for years"—but they were unable to match the Big Red's superlative effort that night. (Cornell Athletic Communications)

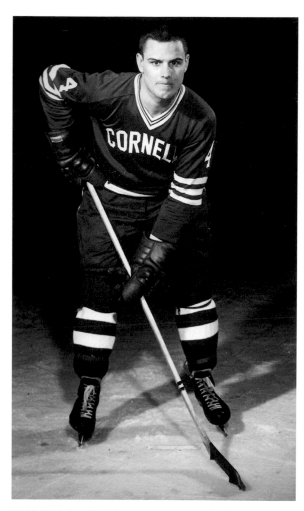

Webb Nichols tallied the game-winning goal in the third period, launching a long shot that eluded Harvard goaltender Godfrey Wood to make it 2–0. The Crimson scored to narrow the lead, but the Big Red defense held firm after that—and the exultant fans spilled onto the ice to carry off the victorious Cornell players. (Cornell Athletic Communications)

Forward Steve Kijanka was one of the three skilled Canadian players who came to Cornell in 1959. As juniors, they were the leaders of Coach Patten's most successful team, which posted a 13–5 record and finished second in the Ivy League—setting the stage for greater accomplishments to come. (Cornell Athletic Communications)

confidence grew as they battled through a scoreless first period. Harvard failed to score despite outshooting Cornell and having a five-on-three advantage for nearly a minute. "We kept them off the scoresheet and started to really believe in ourselves," says Mateka. "Everyone just played out of their skulls. Not just up to our potential—beyond our potential. Kennedy was probably getting tired because he'd already stopped fifteen or twenty shots, but the game was moving along favorably for us."

In the second period, Cornell went on the power play—and scored. Forwards Jerry Kostandoff '64 and Jim Stevens '64 broke into the Harvard zone. Kostandoff sent the puck across the ice to Stevens, who fired a return pass across the goalmouth. Kostandoff deflected it past the Crimson goalie. Lynah erupted—at 12:32 of the second, Cornell led 1–0.

"Harvard, at the beginning of the game, had no reason to be concerned," says Mateka. "They had a great record, and they'd been beating the pants off us for years. But as we got into the game, things started to change a little bit. The dynamics changed." According to Mateka, the Cornell defense was stifling Harvard's talented skaters, checking them closely and forcing a lot of long shots. "Kennedy could stop those with his eyes closed. Anything from long distance—if he had a chance to see it, he had it."

The second period ended 1–0. The volume level rose in Lynah as the teams took the ice for the final twenty minutes, and the Cornell players continued to play "out of their skulls." And then a seemingly routine dump-in stunned the Harvard players. "In the third period, Webb Nichols '63 scored on a long shot from center ice," recalls Mateka. "I was on the ice behind

Team captain Marty Tormey, a senior, had endured defeats by Harvard in previous seasons by such scores as 9–0 and 12–2. He was overjoyed by the tremendous effort put forth by his teammates in this 1962 victory. (Cornell Athletic Communications)

Cornell Hockey Team Skates Past Harvard

By KENNY VAN SICKLE

The town and gown and the hinterlands are still buzzing today over Saturday night's sports spectacular on East Hill, the Cornell hockey team's 2-1 victory over Harvard before 4,200 bug-eyed fans in Lynah Rink.

The Redmen triumphed at what seemed like great odds, handing Harvard its first Ivy League loss in two seasons or 13 games.

And Laing Kennedy, everybody's choice for "puckster of the night" or "puckster of the year," nearly shut 'em out.

Except for a brief moment in the third period, when the Redmen may have let up a little at ice leading 2-0, Kennedy stopped everything. He had 48 saves. And the defense guys in front of him gave him excellent support. After

record, but it has only three contests left, two with Brown and one with Princeton.

Harvard's only other loss to an Easterner this season was to Clarkson. It is now 11-4 overall and Cornell is 8-4. Harvard lost a pair to Minnesota in the Mid-West during the mid-year recess. Cornell, with six matches left, easily is having its best season since 1910 when it was 10-0. It plays at Colgate Tuesday.

Many of Kennedy's 48 saves bordered on the impossible. He was all over, and sometimes left the net to make recoveries. He held Harvard to its lowest output of the season. Its other low-goal games were a 2-0 victory over St. Lawrence and a 7-2 loss to Minnesota.

Wood is listed as Harvard's No. 2 tender but he has played as much this year as All-Ivy League goalie Bob Bland. Bland sat it out because in practice here Friday night he caught a puck over his right eye and seven stitches were needed to close it. Bland came here with a 2.5 goal average; Wood with 2.3.

Cincinnati coach Cooney Weiland removed Goalie Wood with 38 seconds left. At that stage Patten countered by flooding the rink with defensemen. During those hectic moments a curious play came up. Cornell was called for icing the puck. Usually the face-off is in the territory of the team doing the icing. This time the officials called for the face-off at center ice many eyebrows were raised. The officials pointed out later that it was an error that they had called "icing," because of a technicality of "an 'appointed' goalie (Harry Howell) being on the ice." And when there is a mistake the face-off is at the center.

That didn't matter much to Cornell's No. 1 fan, Bill Stowe, leading cheers near the penalty box. But Harvard coach Weiland was noticeably perturbed!

Miss Joy Barnard, one of the Lynah Rink figure skating professionals, delighted the crowd with her number between periods.

The Princeton Frosh beat the Cornell youngsters, 8-3, in the preliminary. Gloves were all over the ice and fists were swung in the last minute. But no blows landed enough to draw blood.

FULL HOUSE: Lynah Rink had them sitting in the aisles match. The Cantabs have the puck in this photo and are

LAING KENNEDY
Tends Nets

Ive Ikauniks, sophomore wing, shook off a Red defender and skated in on Laing the Red braced themselves and fought off all challenges.

The Redmen had a little luck, too, for Harvard "made a real effort out of every body, all in one evening."

Having observed the Cantabs

men was convinced that his gang would be up against three lines of really fast skaters. So he was tickled to see "our kids stay close to them all the way, in fact skate with them at times."

"Harvard is as good a skating club as I have seen in a long time," said Patten, who came here from St. Lawrence six years ago."

Cornell got its first goal at 12:32 of the second period when Harvard was down a man. It was a 10-foot rebound by Jerry Kostandoff, on a pass from Jim Stevens. The second was at 8:02 of the third and Webb Nichols' 30-foot angle backhand loft shot found the netting. Goalie Godfrey Wood, trying to field it on the short hop like a baseball shortstop, couldn't come up with it.

The place had been a bedlam after the first Cornell tally. It was worse after the second. And at the game's end the students really went berserk, invading the ice to shoulder off their heroes. The rink's clock was signal enough to indicate the end, for the buzzer couldn't be heard in the din.

The fact that it was Cornell's first victory over Harvard in hockey in 51 years is incidental. For it was only the 15th game in a series that began in 1909-10. The last victory, in 1911 in Boston, was 3-2.

Harvard had't lost in the league since the final game of the 1960 season when it bowed to Yale. It was tied by Yale in the finale last year when it won the title with 0-1. Harvard still has a good chance to repeat as titlist for it is there 2-1.

Cornell still leads the league on a point basis with 8 on a 4-3

SCORING
First Period
None.
Penalties—C. Oliver, 1:58; C. Mateka, 2:50; H. Taylor, 5:03; H, Heintzman, 7:37; H, Kinasewich, 9:42.
Second Period
1. C—Kostandoff (Stevens) 12:32
Penalties—C, Walker, 7:06; H, Kinasewich, 11:48; H, Taylor, 19:01.
Third Period
2. C—Nichle (unassisted) 8:02
3. H—Ikauniks (Howell) 8:02
Penalty—H, Ikauniks, 7:47.

Red Polo

Hill Teams Take Four Victories

Cornell polo trios annexed a quartet of victories over the weekend.

The highlight was the varsity's 14-11 decision over Yale in the Riding Hall. Behind at half-time, 8-5, Cornell spurted in the third period to leap ahead and it held on firmly in the final canto. Frank Butterworth led Cornell with seven goals while George Lenher batted home five for the Elis.

Cornell jayvees beat the Yale spares at New Haven, 14-7, with Bernardo Herrerra scoring six goals.

A combination frosh - jayvee team won two matches Friday and Saturday at Culver (Ind.) Military Academy, 12-9, and 15-12. Pal Dix was the Red pacesetter.

Groton Matmen Call Off Meet

Groton High's wrestling team has so many boys out sick that it had to forego its trip to Hamilton Saturday for a meet with Hamilton High School. The meet was cancelled.

Groton has two meets this week, at Dryden at 6:30 p.m. Wednesday and at Homer on Friday.

COLLEGE HOCKEY
St. Lawrence 5, Ottawa 1.
Colgate 4, Army 1.
Colby 6, RPI 3.

Home Teams Win in NBA

By The Associated Press

It was a right nice weekend for the home boys in the National Basketball Association. Four games were played Saturday and four Sunday with the home clubs winning six.

The St. Louis Hawks were the only home losers, dropping a 127-124 decision to the Los Angeles Lakers Saturday and a 121-113 encounter to the Pistons at Detroit Sunday.

Philadelphia, winner of 10 of its last 12 games, split a pair with Syracuse, losing 134-112 on the Nats' court Saturday and winning 128-117 at home Sunday. Boston's division leading Celtics downed New York 130-114 in a home game Sunday. The Knicks, however, won at home Saturday, beating the Cincinnati Royals 121-110. The Packers surprised the Lakers Sunday, winning 113-105 at Chicago.

Wilt Chamberlain hit 50 points or more for the 39th time this season in Sunday's foul-filled game with the Nats. The 50 points upped his total for 60 games to 2,980.

Bob Leonard, scoring 18 of his 24 points in the second half, sparked the Packers to their upset of the Lakers. Gene Shue came through with 30 points and Don Ohl with 25 as the Pistons tightened their hold on third place in the Western Division.

Pro Basketball
By The Associated Press

NATIONAL BASKETBALL ASSO.
Eastern Division

	W.	L.	Pct.	G.B.
Boston	42	13	.764	—
Philadelphia	37	23	.617	7½
Syracuse	27	31	.466	16½
New York	20	36	.357	22½

Western Division

	W.	L.	Pct.	G.B.
Los Angeles	42	17	.712	—
Cincinnati	31	26	.544	10
Detroit	26	32	.448	15½
St. Louis	21	37	.362	20½
Chicago	12	43	.218	28

Saturday's Results
Syracuse 134, Philadelphia 112
Detroit 116, Chicago 109
Los Angeles 127, St. Louis 124
New York 121, Cincinnati 110
Sunday's Results
Boston 130, New York 114
Philadelphia 128, Syracuse 117
Chicago 113, Los Angeles 105
Detroit 121, St. Louis 113
Monday's Games
Cincinnati vs Los Angeles at Morgantown, W.Va.
Boston at Chicago
Tuesday's Games
Chicago vs Syracuse at New York
Los Angeles at New York
Detroit at Cincinnati
Boston at St. Louis

AMERICAN LEAGUE
Eastern Division

	W.	L.	Pct.	G.B.
Pittsburgh	8	9	.471	—
Chicago	6	7	.462	—
New York	5	8	.385	1
Cleveland	3	8	.273	2

Western Division

	W.	L.	Pct.	G.B.
San Francisco	9	2	.818	—
Kansas City	8	4	.667	1½
Hawaii	5	6	.455	4

Saturday's Results
Cleveland 120, Chicago 114
San Francisco 113, New York 109
Hawaii 100, Kansas City 91
Sunday's Results
New York 112, Cleveland 109
Chicago 109, San Francisco 107
Kansas City 105, Hawaii 92
Monday's Games
No games scheduled
Tuesday's Games
Kansas City vs Hawaii at San Diego
San Francisco vs Cleveland at Sandusky, Ohio

—Journal Photo by Sol Goldberg
NO. 1: Cornell goalie Laing Kennedy gets a free ride off Lynah Rink ice Saturday night after the Big Red beat Harvard, 2-1, in a big upset. Kennedy had 48 saves.

The Monday after the game, the *Ithaca Journal*'s Kenny Van Sickle reported that area residents were "still buzzing" after Cornell's stunning upset over Harvard on the previous Saturday night. (Courtesy of Rudy Mateka)

him when he airmailed that floater. It went way up, under the lights, came down about a yard in front of the goaltender, and bounced in."

Kennedy recalls this pivotal moment: "Lynah Rink exploded. We were up 2–0 with twelve minutes to go. Coach Patten was really composed, keeping us calm and telling us, 'Okay, keep doing it, keep doing it.'" Tension built when Harvard forward Ike Ikauniks scored at 11:02 of the third period to make it 2–1. "And then all hell broke loose," says Kennedy, recalling the Crimson's frantic offensive outburst. "I'd never seen so much rubber in all my life."

In the final minute, Weiland pulled goalie Wood for an extra attacker. Patten countered by putting five defensemen on the ice. "It was 2–1, and we were hanging on by our teeth," says Marty Tormey '62, the Cornell captain. "Laing was just terrific."

Kennedy stopped everything Harvard threw at him in their final frenzy—and got some help from the pipes, when a shot by the Crimson's Dave Grannis clanged off the left goalpost with forty five seconds remaining. "There was this overwhelm-

ing feeling in the final seconds," recalls the goalie, who made forty-eight saves that night. "We're going to win! We're going to win! I started jumping up and down."

The *Ithaca Journal*'s Kenny Van Sickle recorded the outcome: "The place had been bedlam after the first Cornell tally. It was worse after the second. And at the game's end the students really went berserk, invading the ice to shoulder off their heroes. The rink's clock was signal enough to indicate the end, for the buzzer couldn't be heard in the din."

Kennedy says he probably should have been frightened by the mob climbing over the sideboards—there was netting only behind the goals in those days—but he was caught up in the emotion of winning such an unexpected victory. "They carried me off the ice. It was unbelievable. I've never seen such spontaneous jubilation. I would say that game set the stage for Cornell hockey—for the Lynah Faithful."

The account of the game in the 1962 *Cornellian* called it "the single greatest victory in the history of Cornell hockey." At that point, it was—but even greater victories were to come.

Goaltender Ken Dryden was front and center in the 1966–67 men's hockey team photo. Co-captain Dave Ferguson (12) sits next to him, with the other co-captain, Murray Deathe (18), directly behind; head coach Ned Harkness is on the far left of the second row. (Cornell Athletic Communications)

CORNELL 4, BOSTON UNIVERSITY 1
ONONDAGA COUNTY WAR MEMORIAL, SYRACUSE, NEW YORK, MARCH 18, 1967

After their monumental victory over Harvard, Coach Paul Patten's team concluded the 1961–62 season with a 13–5 record. Patten returned for one more year—with Laing Kennedy as his captain—and Cornell posted a 9–9–1 mark. Patten announced his resignation before the season ended, and he departed Ithaca for a new occupation, owning and operating golf courses.

As athletic director, Bob Kane had to find a new coach. He didn't have to look far. At Rensselaer Polytechnic Institute in nearby Troy, New York, there was an accomplished hockey coach who had won a national championship in 1954. His name was Ned Harkness.

Cornell offered Harkness a better salary than he was being paid at RPI, but he later said that the primary motivating factor was not money—it was the opportunity to team up with Bob Kane, "the best man I ever worked for."

A skillful motivator and tireless recruiter, Harkness quick-ly moved the Big Red program forward. His first two teams had respectable records of 12–10–1 and 19–7, and the 1965–66 squad—featuring many of the Canadian players that Harkness had recruited, including co-captains Doug Ferguson '67 and Mike Doran '67—finished 22–5. In the Eastern College Athletic Conference Tournament, they clobbered Boston College 9–0 and Boston University 8–1 before losing to Clarkson in the championship game. The freshman team, coached by Ned's father, William, had an even better season; led by a tall Canadian goaltender named Ken Dryden, they were undefeated.

When senior goalie Dave Quarrie '67 was injured before the start of the 1966–67 season, Dryden stepped in to take his place in the net. The team was led by an outstanding group of seniors, including Murray Deathe '67 (who spelled his last name without the final "e" in those days), Harry Orr '67, and the Fergusons—twins Doug and Dave and brother Bob (all '67).

An injury to senior Dave Quarrie made Ken Dryden the starting goalie in his sophomore season. His record would be 26–0–1 in the games that he started, posting a goals-against average of 1.46 as he led the Big Red to its first national championship. (Courtesy of the Division of Rare and Manuscript Collections, Cornell University Library)

They started the season with eleven victories in a row, including a 3–2 win over Michigan State, the defending national champion, in the final of the ECAC Holiday Tournament. (In those days, this was a regular event, matching the top teams in the conference against western foes in games played in large venues such as Boston Garden and Madison Square Garden.)

Two weeks later, they battled Boston University through two overtimes in the championship game of another holiday event, the Boston Arena Christmas Tournament. The game ended in a 3–3 tie, and the rivals were named co-champions. "Some of our guys were ticked," recalls Deathe. "They wanted to keep going."

In the Big Red's next game, at Lynah against Yale, Quarrie started in goal instead of Dryden. Cornell had beaten Yale 5–3 in New Haven, so the team may have been a bit overconfident— or maybe they were still thinking about that tie against BU. In any case, they lost, 4–3 in overtime. Cornell bounced back emphatically in their next game, an 8–0 win at Colgate, and then returned to Ithaca to trounce Brown 6–1—the first victory in a sixty-three-game home winning streak at Lynah Rink, a record that will probably never be matched.

The wins continued to pile up. In the ECAC Tournament, Cornell crushed Brown 11–2 in the quarterfinal and demolished Boston College 12–2 in the semi. On March 11, 1967, they

(*facing page*) The all-sophomore line of (left to right) Brian Cornell, Pete Tufford, and Bob McGuinn made a crucial contribution to the Big Red's success in the 1966–67 season. After Brian Cornell was hurt, Ted Coviello— another sophomore—took his place. (Cornell Athletic Communications)

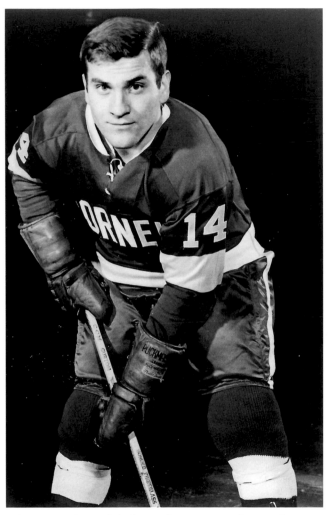

Bob Kinasewich scored the first goal against BU in the 1967 championship game, deflecting a shot from Murray Deathe. They played on
the defense-first third line, so the score was somewhat unexpected—
and a big lift for the Big Red. (Cornell Athletic Communications)

Doug Ferguson took a pass from his twin brother, Dave, to score
the goal that put the Big Red ahead 3–0 in the championship game.
Natives of Birsay, Saskatchewan, the twins were recruited by Harkness
along with their younger brother Bob to come to Cornell as members
of the Class of 1967. (Cornell Athletic Communications)

faced Boston University in the championship game at Boston Garden—and won 4–3. Their record was 25–1–1, and they were unquestionably the best team in the East.

A week later, the NCAA Tournament got under way at the Onondaga County War Memorial in Syracuse. In those days, it was a four-team affair, decided in a weekend. The East was represented by Cornell and BU; the West by North Dakota and Michigan State. Only an hour from Ithaca, the War Memorial was a much friendlier venue than Boston Garden—and the building was packed with fans wearing carnelian and white. "In Syracuse, we had basically a home crowd," says Pete Tufford. "It wasn't like being in Boston. We felt at home."

The Big Red faced the green-clad squad from North Dakota in the semifinal. Despite Cornell's record, many hockey followers expected a victory by the Fighting Sioux. Since the start of the national tournament in 1948, only two eastern teams had won—Boston College in 1949 and RPI, coached by Harkness, in 1954. "There was an aura about the western teams," says Deathe, "and we hadn't had much luck against them. We had lost to Denver twice [in 1965–66], and when we were sophomores, Michigan clobbered us [7–1 on January 2, 1965]."

The game was tight, with both teams checking relentlessly and the officials calling numerous penalties. The Big Red got on the board at 17:27 of the first period on a goal by defenseman Walter "Skip" Stanowski '68. He had been sent off for boarding and was just returning to the ice. "I was coming out of the [penalty] box," Stanowski told the *Ithaca Journal*'s Jerry Langdon after the game, "when I saw the puck just bouncing off [forward Bob McGuinn's] stick at center ice. I was going to

go to our bench, but the puck was there so I took off."

Streaking into the offensive zone on a breakaway, Stanowski launched a long shot that went over the shoulder of goalie Mike Curran. North Dakota disputed the goal, saying that Stanowski should have returned to the Cornell blue line before advancing, but the officials ruled that it was legal pass from McGuinn and the 1–0 score held up.

It was the only goal of the game. Despite numerous scoring chances for both teams, the goalies stopped everything. Curran finished the game with forty-one saves and Dryden—standing tall—had thirty. "Our whole defense was tremendous," said Harkness after the game. "And what more can I say about Kenny Dryden in the goal? He's the reason we're here."

The BU Terriers defeated Michigan State in the other semi, and the stage was set for a rematch of the ECAC title game—this time for the national championship. "Even though our games with BU had been close," says Deathe, "I can recall feeling pretty confident before the game." Tufford concurs. "With BU we just plugged away," he says. "I don't recall that there was ever any fear. We expected to win."

Dryden says that he had a certain degree of apprehension, perhaps natural for a goaltender, because of his respect for BU as an opponent. "They were always strong," he says. "They had talented players. They had good goaltending and a great coach, Jack Kelley. They were always difficult to beat—and you always knew you had gone through something when you played BU."

The championship game broke quickly in Cornell's favor. Early in the opening period, Deathe took a pass from Stanowski and launched a shot toward the Terrier goal. His linemate Bob

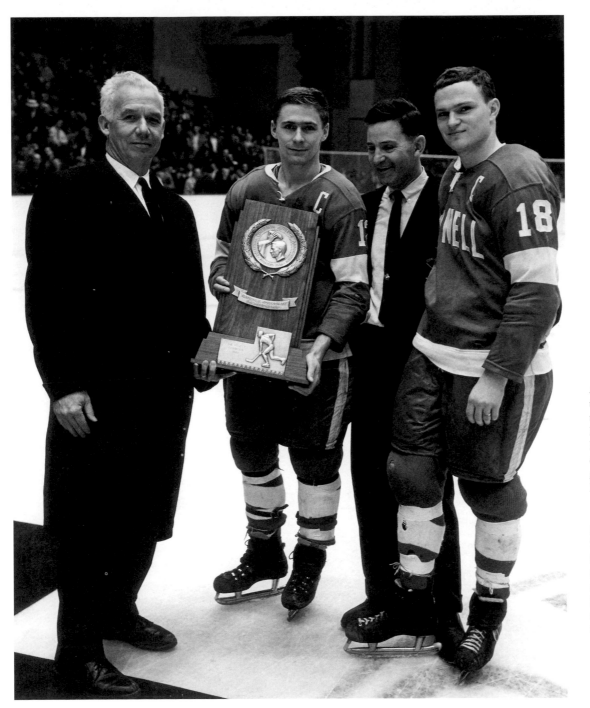

After Cornell defeated BU to win the NCAA title, the championship trophy was presented to Ned Harkness and co-captains Dave Ferguson and Murray Deathe. The coach praised his players as a "truly great hockey team." (Cornell Athletic Communications)

(*facing page*) The NCAA All-Tournament Team honored four Cornell players (left to right): Mike Doran, Harry Orr, Skip Stanowski, and Ken Dryden. They were joined by Boston University's Jim Quinn and Michigan State's Tom Mikkola. (Cornell Athletic Communications)

In the NCAA semifinal, North Dakota goalie Mike Curran stopped a shot by Bob McGuinn, one of his forty-one saves in the game. Cornell won 1–0 to advance to the championship final. (© *Cornell Daily Sun,* used by permission)

In the NCAA final against Boston University, Ken Dryden gave up a single goal—the only one he allowed on seventy-two shots that weekend. Here he prepares to make a save, flanked by Bruce Pattison (21) and Skip Stankowski (3). (© *Cornell Daily Sun,* used by permission)

Kinasewich '67 deflected it past goalie Wayne Ryan, and the Big Red was ahead 1–0. "We were the third line," says Deathe. "We were supposed to keep the other team off the scoreboard—that was what we were known for. So when we scored that first goal, that was a big goal for us."

The two teams battled back and forth for the rest of the period, and at 17:40 BU forward—and future head coach of the Terriers—Jack Parker was sent to the penalty box for hooking. On the power play, Harry Orr fed Stanowski at the point, and his thirty-foot shot went over Ryan's shoulder. The Big Red was up 2–0 as the buzzer sounded.

In the second period, things were looking up for BU when two Cornell players were sent to the penalty box, but the defense held firm during the five-on-three. And then, at 12:41, the Big Red scored on another power play, when Dave Ferguson fed his brother Doug, who beat Ryan. At 3–0, the game appeared to be locked up—but BU scored twelve seconds later, on a short shot by Mike Sobeski. The period ended 3–1.

As the third period began, the Lynah Faithful roared as the Big Red took the ice. They knew the next few minutes would be crucial. "BU would have had some hope remaining," says Dryden. "It's a 3–1 game, and you have the feeling that if you can just get the next goal and make it 3–2, then everything is up for grabs." Things looked good for the Terriers when referee Bill Cleary—who had played for Harvard and would later coach the Crimson team for nineteen years—sent off Orr for spearing, a major penalty. BU would be on the power play for the next five minutes. ("The Big Red partisans chanted, 'Cleary is a bum,'" reported the *Journal*'s Langdon.)

The Big Red fans urged on their penalty killers, and BU didn't score—"this seemed to take the starch out of the Terriers," wrote Langdon. Then, at 10:22, Bob McGuinn '69 knocked in a rebound, with assists going to Ted Coviello '69 and Stanowski. Cornell was up 4–1. "That was the real crushing one," says Dryden.

McGuinn doesn't recall the play clearly. "I think it was a backhand shot," he says. "What I do remember is coming back to the bench after scoring the goal. Skip Stanowski turned to me and said, 'We're golden now.'"

With the outcome all but determined, the game got rough. "It was a little feisty at the end," says Tufford. "They were getting frustrated, and there were a couple of tussles." Doug Ferguson got into it with Bill Riley and Jack Parker—he was hit with a five-minute major penalty, while the BU players received two-minute penalties for high-sticking and roughing, respectively. It didn't matter. The game ended, and the Cornell hockey team had won its first NCAA title.

Co-captains Murray Deathe and Dave Ferguson accepted the championship trophy after the game. Skip Stanowski—who had two goals and two assists—was named the Most Valuable Player, and he joined teammates Doran, Dryden, and Orr on the All-Tournament Team. In retrospect, it seems remarkable that Dryden was not named the MVP after allowing only one goal on seventy-two shots in the two games. "As a goalie, yes, that's about as good as it gets," he says. "But [Stanowski] being in on four of the five goals as a defenseman and scoring the only goal in the first game, that's an even bigger statistic."

As the horn sounded to mark the end of the final, Ned Harkness and the Big Red players began their celebration of Cornell's first NCAA hockey championship. (© *Cornell Daily Sun*, used by permission)

The day after the game, Ned Harkness recalled that his father, who had died three years earlier, had predicted that his freshman team of 1963–64 would go on to win a national championship. "Pop would have been proud of these boys," he said. "They are truly a great hockey team."

✧ NED HARKNESS, MOTIVATOR ✧

© *Cornell Daily Sun*, used by permission

In the semifinal game of the Syracuse Holiday Tournament my senior year, we beat a good Minnesota-Duluth team with an excellent goaltender by the name of Chico Resch, 2–1 in overtime. St. Lawrence beat Colgate in the semifinal, and we therefore had to play St. Lawrence in the Saturday night final.

We were all prepared to go home for Christmas three or four days after the game before resuming our regular schedule the next weekend. At the end of the second period we found ourselves down 3–0 to a fired-up St. Lawrence team we had beaten easily earlier in the year. Ned came into the locker room after the second period in a rage. The extra sticks were lined up behind the door and were soon heaved all over the floor. Two garbage cans hit the wall. The only thing he said was, "If we lose this game we will be practicing at Lynah all next week, and don't believe for a minute that any of you are going anyplace but back to Ithaca."

By the six-minute mark of the third period we had scored four goals and had a fifth goal disallowed. We won the game 4–3. To this day, I am not sure whether he was really serious or not, but I don't believe any one of us wanted to test him.

PETE TUFFORD

Doug Ferguson watches the action in the semifinal, getting ready for his next shift on the ice. In the final against BU, he would take a pass from his twin brother, Dave, to score Cornell's third goal. (© *Cornell Daily Sun*, used by permission)

National Champions! An exultant Ned Harkness charges onto the ice with his team after the final buzzer of the NCAA championship game. (© *Cornell Daily Sun*, used by permission)

The head coach celebrates the 1970 NCAA championship with his seniors (left to right): John Hughes, Dan Lodboa, Gordie Lowe, Garth Ryan, Steve Giuliani, and Dick Bertrand. (Jim Cunningham '71/Cornell Athletic Communications)

CORNELL 6, CLARKSON 4
OLYMPIC ARENA, LAKE PLACID, NEW YORK, MARCH 21, 1970

In the final game of 1969–70, Cornell was on the verge of what many considered an impossible achievement: an undefeated season. But with one period remaining in the NCAA championship game against Clarkson, the score was tied. The Golden Knights had scored first in the game, and their goalie, Bruce Bullock, was stopping one Cornell shot after another. The scoreboard read 3–3 as the Big Red players took the ice. The overwhelmingly pro-Cornell crowd in Olympic Arena was excited but on edge—unaware that they were about to witness one of the greatest individual efforts in the history of college hockey.

After winning the NCAA championship in 1967, Cornell had appeared poised to do it again the following year. Many of the key players, including Ken Dryden, were back for another season—and they were all well conditioned and well schooled in the relentless forechecking style emphasized by Ned Harkness.

After a surprising early season loss to Brown, the team ran off twenty-three wins in a row, capping it with a 6–3 victory over Boston College for the ECAC championship. The Big Red advanced to the NCAA Tournament with high hopes—but North Dakota avenged their semifinal loss from the year before, winning 3–1. A day later, Cornell downed BC in the consolation game 6–1 to end the season 27–2.

The 1968–69 team was again a powerhouse, and their season unfolded in much the same way, with an early loss—this time to RPI, in overtime—followed by a long string of victories. In the ECAC Tournament at Boston Garden, the Big Red edged Boston University 3–2 in overtime to advance to the championship game against Harvard. They won the title again, 4–2, and geared up for another shot at the NCAA title.

The games were held at the Broadmoor World Arena in Colorado Springs, Colorado. In the semifinal, Cornell topped

Before the 1969–70 season, Ned Harkness posed at Lynah Rink with his three captains (left to right): John Hughes, Dick Bertrand, and Dan Lodboa. (Cornell Athletic Communications)

Michigan Tech 4–3 in overtime. One game remained, against the defending national champion, Denver. The Pioneers had crushed Harvard 9–2 in their semi.

Harkness reportedly considered resting Dryden, who was exhausted after the overtime game the night before—but how could he? It would be his final game in the Cornell goal, capping a brilliant career in which he had been named All-American three years in a row.

Unfortunately, Denver prevailed, winning a hard-fought 4–3 game to secure their second title in a row. Cornell once again had a 27–2 record, but Harkness was bitterly disappointed. "We're standing around on the ice after the [championship] game," recalls forward Garth Ryan '70, "and Ned had this look on his face. His eyes were full of tears and his lips were quivering. He looked at us and said, 'We'll ram it down their [expletive] throats next season.' He was mad as hell. So we thought, *OK, the next season has started.*"

With the graduation of four All-Americans—Dryden, Tufford, Bruce Pattison '69, and Brian Cornell '69—it was widely expected that 1969–70 would be a rebuilding season for Harkness's team. Ryan says, "I remember an article where a coach of one of the other teams in the league said, 'Now we'll see how good they are without Dryden.'"

The new goalie was Brian Cropper '71, who stood 5'6", at most, and played a very different style from the 6'4" Dryden, making acrobatic moves to stop pucks and earning the affectionate nickname Brian "The Stopper" Cropper. (He was also referred to as the "Little Kid," in contrast to the "Big Kid" who had preceded him.) Cropper had been used sparingly as

With the graduation of Ken Dryden, junior Brian Cropper took over as the starting goalie. Almost a foot shorter than his predecessor, "The Stopper" had an acrobatic style that was very effective, as seen by his 1.86 goals-against average for the season. (Cornell Athletic Communications)

Senior tri-captain John Hughes was a team leader and outstanding goal scorer. In his three years as varsity player, he would put the puck in the opposition net sixty-eight times. Later, as a graduate student, he would join teammate Bill Duthie to coach Cornell's first women's varsity hockey team. (Cornell Athletic Communications)

Brian McCutcheon played on the first line with John Hughes and Kevin Pettit. They were one of the most effective combinations in Cornell hockey history, scoring a combined total of more than four hundred points. McCutcheon would later return to Lynah Rink as head coach of the Big Red from 1987 to 1995. (Cornell Athletic Communications)

Dryden's backup in 1968–69, mostly in mop-up time at the end of one-sided Cornell wins.

If the hockey pundits were skeptical about Cornell's prospects, the coach wasn't. "I remember the first meeting we had with Ned before the season began," says winger Brian McCutcheon '71. "He very emphatically said that we would win the national championship. That set the tone for the year—from the get-go, there was great confidence."

Cornell started strong, scoring twenty goals as they posted big wins in their first three games. On December 6, 1969, they narrowly escaped an upset by Brown, when defenseman Dan Lodboa '70 scored in overtime to secure a 5–4 win.

Lodboa had been a forward when he came to Cornell, but Harkness converted him to defense—a brilliant move that was a key to his team's success. Lodboa—"Bo" to his teammates—was an extraordinary skater and stickhandler, with a knack for stealing pucks and taking off on breakaways. And he had a quick, hard shot, one that frequently sailed over the shoulders or outstretched gloves of startled goalies. In his eighty-seven games at Cornell, Lodboa had fifty-two goals and eighty-two assists. He was the epitome of an offensive defenseman, the first man in on many rushes. Harkness once called him "the Bobby Orr of college hockey."

The first line of the 1969–70 team had John Hughes '70 at center, flanked by Kevin Pettit '71 and McCutcheon. They terrorized opponents, scoring almost at will, and recording a combined total of more than four hundred points in their collegiate careers. The second line—with Ryan, Dick Bertrand '70, and Larry Fullan '72—was almost as deadly, and Harkness rolled two more lines. Most other teams played only three lines, so Cornell's fresh legs were an advantage that allowed them to keep the puck in the offensive zone for long stretches.

After the close call at Brown, the Big Red kept on winning. They were invincible at Lynah, and they closed out 1969 with a 7–2 victory over St. Lawrence in the ECAC Holiday Tournament to finish the first part of the season 9–0. When Cornell began the ECAC Tournament in March, their record was 24–0. They vanquished St. Lawrence 6–1 in the quarterfinal at Lynah. Up next was Harvard in the semifinal at Boston Garden; Cornell prevailed 6–5.

On the next night, they faced Clarkson for the ECAC championship. In a game that the *Ithaca Journal*'s Jerry Langdon termed "spine-tingling," the Big Red won 3–2. The all-sophomore fourth line of Ed Ambis '72, Doug Stewart '72, and Craig Brush '72 made a key contribution, not only playing effective defense but scoring a goal at 12:38 of the second period. Stewart's shot was stopped by Clarkson goalie Bruce Bullock, but Ambis was right there for the rebound that tied the score at 2–2. It was his first goal of the season. Hughes took it from there, scoring twice in the game's final minute. The first goal was disallowed because of an offsides call ("a hairline decision," Harkness said), and Hughes smashed his stick on the ice in disgust. He got a new stick and scored again at 19:46. Game over: 27–0 and on to the NCAA Tournament for the fourth year in a row.

The opponent in the semifinal at Olympic Arena in Lake Placid was Wisconsin, a tough western squad with an outstanding goalie, Wayne Thomas. The Badgers were coached by Bob Johnson, who would win 367 games in his fifteen years at Wis-

Dan Lodboa was a forward who was converted to defense by Ned Harkness. Taken aback by the idea at first, Lodboa became a brilliant offensive defenseman—and his hat trick in the 1970 NCAA championship game is still celebrated as one of the greatest individual performances in college hockey history. (Cornell Athletic Communications)

The marquee at Lake Placid's Olympic Arena welcomed Cornell, Clarkson, Wisconsin, and Michigan Tech to the 1970 NCAA Hockey Tournament. (Jim Cunningham '71/Cornell Athletic Communications)

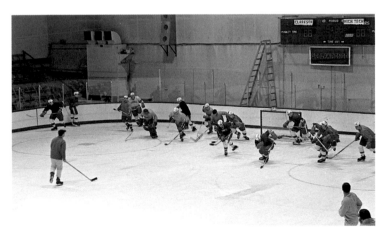

With the scoreboard set for the semifinal game between Clarkson and Michigan Tech, Ned Harkness put his team through the paces on the Olympic Arena ice. At the time, no one knew this was the last practice he would direct as Cornell's head coach. (Jim Cunningham '71/Cornell Athletic Communications)

consin. His team struck first, getting a first-period goal on a power play. There was no scoring in the second, but Cornell was dominating possession; Cropper had only three saves while Thomas had to make twelve. The trend continued into the third, as "Cornell swarmed over Wisconsin," in Langdon's words. At 5:32, Ryan got the tying goal—and then the third line put Cornell ahead, on a goal by Bill Duthie '71. "I was right in front of the net," he recalls. "It only made it over the line by about eight inches, because [Thomas] got part of it and it just trickled in."

The game ended 2–1, and Johnson summed it up by saying, "Their checking was just too much." The box score confirms that evaluation, as it shows that Cropper made only one save in the third period. (The Cornell skaters insist that there were no shots on goal in that period—and Cropper says he doesn't remember.) The Cornell goalie had fifteen saves for the game while Thomas made thirty-six. "All season, we were trying to protect Cropper the best we could," says Duthie. "That game was just an extension of it."

Hughes believes that the NCAA semifinal was the team's finest overall performance. "I remember that as being the best team effort that we ever had," he says. "It didn't matter who was on the ice—Wisconsin didn't get out of their end. And it was just a matter of time before Thomas would let one in. That set us up pretty well for the next night, knowing we could put forth that kind of effort."

In the other semifinal, Clarkson defeated Michigan Tech. So—as had been the case in the 1967 NCAA final—Cornell would be facing the team it had just defeated for the ECAC title a week before for the national championship. Tri-captain

Bertrand, unable to play in the tournament because of NCAA eligibility rules, was up in the press box, serving as color man for Sam Woodside on the radio broadcast. Dave Westner '72 took his place on the second line. Olympic Arena was packed to its two-thousand-seat capacity (and beyond) for the game, and the Lynah Faithful dominated the cheering. Ryan says he has vivid memories of the way it sounded. "The support was tremendous," he says.

The game didn't start well for Cornell. Only twenty seconds into the first period, Clarkson's Luc St. Jean tallied the first goal on a two-on-one break. Four minutes later, Fullan evened the score, taking a pass from Steve Giuliani '70—another forward who had been converted to defense by Harkness—and beating Bullock. Then, with Clarkson's Wayne LaChance in the penalty box for tripping, Ryan put Cornell ahead with an unassisted tally. Late in the period, Hughes was sent off for high-sticking. When Ron Simpson '72 was also penalized twenty-six seconds later, Clarkson had a five-on-three. It didn't take them long to score, and the score was 2–2 as the buzzer sounded. Cornell's forecheck was not as dominant as it had been against Wisconsin, and the Golden Knights were primed for an upset.

"Between periods, I was down in the dressing room with Ned, talking to the players about what Clarkson was doing and what we had to do," says Bertrand. "It worked because we had the right chemistry. We didn't have any superstars. We had great players like Lodboa and Hughes, but everybody made a contribution. The chemistry was there, and Ned pushed the right buttons."

At 3:14 of the second period, the Golden Knights went up

✵ COACH-IN-TRAINING ✵

Some accounts state that Dick Bertrand could not play in the 1970 NCAA Tournament because of his age, but that was not the case. He was older than his teammates, having served as a Toronto policeman for several years before being admitted to Cornell at the age of twenty-five—but the problem was an NCAA rule, not his age. Bertrand explains: "After your twentieth birthday, every year that you played organized hockey counted as a year of eligibility. I had played a year of organized hockey in Canada after my twentieth birthday, so that counted against me." At the time, freshmen were not allowed to play varsity hockey, so players had three years of eligibility. Bertrand had played in the NCAAs in both 1968 and 1969, so he was declared ineligible in 1970. But the experience of watching his teammates and counseling them between periods would prove to be beneficial to him the following year.

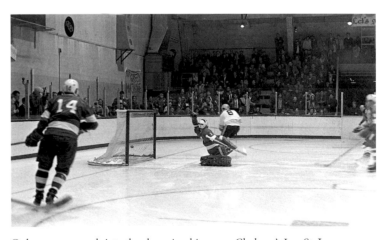

Only twenty seconds into the championship game, Clarkson's Luc St. Jean scores on a two-on-one break to put the Golden Knights ahead 1–0. (Jim Cunningham '71/Cornell Athletic Communications)

During a pause in the action, Garth Ryan surveys the ice. Playing on an injured leg, he would make a poke-check in the third period that would lead to Dan Lodboa's game-winning goal. (Jim Cunningham '71/Cornell Athletic Communications)

3–2 when Bill O'Flaherty knocked in a rebound. Clarkson held the lead for ten minutes, and then Westner tipped a Fullan shot past Bullock to knot the score at 3–3. The second period ended with the game still tied.

The stage was set. Twenty minutes remained. Four minutes into the third, Clarkson's Steve Warr was sent off for tripping Ryan. The Big Red's power play unit took the ice, with Lodboa at the left point. It didn't take long for McCutcheon to find him, and the speedy defenseman broke toward the goal. He fired a shot past Bullock, and Cornell took the lead 4–3.

At 6:01, Westner was called for tripping and Clarkson went on the power play. It got worse a minute and forty-one seconds later, when Gordie Lowe '70 was called for cross-checking. Clarkson had scored easily on their first five-on-three opportunity, and Cornell's lead was clearly in jeopardy. It was, as Langdon wrote, a "golden opportunity."

Cornell's penalty killers spread out, trying to prevent a pass inside that would lead to an easy goal. And then Ryan saw something. "There was a play around the blue line, and their defenseman was reaching for the puck," he recalls. "I poke-checked it ahead, and Lodboa was right on it. I don't know how he anticipated that. He just charged for it and was gone."

Lodboa streaked down the ice on a breakaway and put a shot past Bullock, stick-side. Incredibly, he had scored a shorthanded goal with his team *two men* down—in the last period of the last game of the year, with an undefeated season and a national championship on the line. At 7:58 of the third period, Cornell was up 5–3.

Lodboa wasn't quite done. Five minutes later, he took a pass

With Clarkson leading late in the second period, Dave Westner tips a Larry Fullan shot past goalie Bruce Bullock to tie the score. (Jim Cunningham '71/Cornell Athletic Communications)

With Cornell holding a precarious 4–3 lead and trying to kill a five-on-three, Garth Ryan tipped the puck to Dan Lodboa, who broke into the Clarkson zone and put the puck past Bruce Bullock, sending the Lynah Faithful into ecstasy. (Jim Cunningham '71/Cornell Athletic Communications)

✛ THE HARKNESS SYSTEM ✛

The players on the 1969–70 team are quick to praise Ned Harkness for both his motivational skills and the style of play he taught them. Knowing that he had an exceptional group of skaters, Harkness emphasized puck possession and control of the offensive zone. "It was a four-man attack," says Brian McCutcheon, who would go on to coach the Cornell team from 1987 to 1995. "Ned had converted two forwards into defensemen, Dan Lodboa and Steve Giuliani—excellent puck carriers, puck handlers, passers. That was Ned's philosophy: get a defenseman not only to move the puck out of the zone but also to join the rush. And in Lodboa's case, he'd lead the rush. I don't recall any other teams doing it in those days. To Ned's credit, he was ahead of the game at that point."

At first, Lodboa was not happy with his new role. "I didn't know what to think, to be honest," he says, recalling the moment when Harkness told him about his change of position. "I was upset. I called my father at home and said, 'He wants me to be a defenseman.' And my father said, 'Well, you're at Cornell University because of one man.' And then Ned Harkness took me on the ice every day after practice, telling me how you play different situations. He told me, 'I've got to have you back there [on defense] because you're my best puck handler.'"

Once his attackers had moved the puck into the offensive zone, Harkness wanted it to stay there. "Our practices were harder than our games, so we were in great shape," says McCutcheon. "And as I look back, I don't know how often we even practiced our defensive zone coverage. It was forecheck, forecheck, forecheck. And when we got into games, it was our belief that if we just kept doing this, eventually it would turn out in our favor."

Bill Duthie confirms that the team's relentless style was a product of their hard work in practice. "One thing we prided ourselves on was conditioning," he says. "I can remember talking to guys on the other team during games. The third period would be starting and we're at the faceoff, and they would say, 'How do you guys keep going?' I'd just point over to the bench: 'That guy over there.'"

Harkness's relentless four-man attack required quick adjustments. "A thing that we spent a lot of time on in practice was that if you have a defenseman going in, one of the wingers has to come back and cover that defensive spot," says Brian Cropper. "Ned would be blowing his whistle all day long. He'd see one defenseman on the blue line with guys forechecking, and he'd say, 'OK, who's covering the other point?' Because all of a sudden you could get a two-on-one or a three-on-one against you."

That rarely happened—but when it did, Cropper was ready to stop it. "He was a crucial guy," says John Hughes. "He was always there when we needed him." Cropper played in all twenty-nine games. His backup was Bob Rule '71, an All-American lacrosse goalie with little hockey experience. Rule played very little—parts of three games, for a total of thirty-seven minutes in the entire season. "Brian was amazing," says Hughes. "It wasn't like he could have an off game and we could put somebody else out there. The pressure was on him all the time."

It was an unbeatable combination: great skaters in top condition, a four-man attack, relentless forechecking, quick defensive adjustments, and an outstanding goalie—skillfully guided by a coach who knew exactly how to motivate every one of his players. "Ned was a phenomenal coach," says Cropper. "You loved him or hated him, and you could do both within an hour. Ned could get so mad at you, and then half an hour later he'd come up behind you and give you a tap on the pads—and you knew everything was OK."

from McCutcheon on a three-on-one break and completed his hat trick. "I broke down the wing and walked right in on Bullock," he says. Lodboa fired another hard shot, stick-side: "I said, Here's the same thing—stop it if you can."

Bullock couldn't. The Big Red led 6–3, and an ear-splitting chant of "Twenty-nine and O! Twenty-nine and O!" rattled the walls of the arena. Clarkson would score one more goal, but Lodboa had put the game out of reach with his spectacular effort. It ended 6–4. "The last game was Danny's night," says Hughes. "He was unbelievable." Unsurprisingly, Lodboa was named the Most Valuable Player of the tournament.

"After the game, some reporter asked me, 'What was the strategy going into the third period?'" recalls Ryan with a chuckle. "I said, 'Give the puck to Bo.' He was something else."

At that point, Ryan was barely able to stand. He had been injured in a game several weeks earlier, when a hard hit to his leg had caused nerve damage. "In the first practice after that, every time I tried to turn I would fall down," he says. "My ankle just wouldn't hold me." Ryan had to play the last few games with his ankle heavily taped to keep it from collapsing. "And then I got blindsided again, in the last five minutes [of the championship game]," he says. "Tore my knee up, and I had to be operated on. So while all of the other guys were out celebrating during the week after we won, I was in the hospital in a full-length cast."

The Big Red players were hailed as heroes when they

The scoreboard says it all: time has expired and Cornell leads Clarkson 6–4. The Big Red have won the national championship and completed an unprecedented 29–0 season. (Jim Cunningham '71/Cornell Athletic Communications)

returned to campus, and more than three hundred people jammed the annual Ithaca Hockey Boosters banquet, including university president Dale Corson, board of trustees chairman Robert Purcell, and athletic director Bob Kane. Ithaca mayor Hunna Johns proclaimed Cornell Hockey Week, saying, "The Cornell hockey team and its coach, Ned Harkness, have been an inspiration to the community."

As the Cornell players gather on the ice to celebrate their victory, the Lynah Faithful and the pep band look on, exhausted and elated, as one fan raises his camera to capture the moment. (Jim Cunningham '71/Cornell Athletic Communications)

(*right*) After the final buzzer sounds, captains Dan Lodboa and John Hughes celebrate the culmination of their unmatched season. (Cornell Athletic Communications)

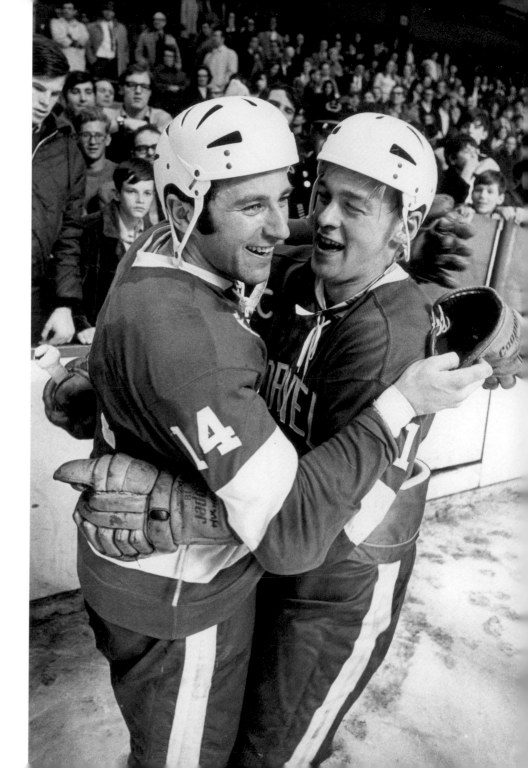

We're number one: Ned Harkness and his captains pose for a photo with the NCAA championship trophy, which rests in the arms of Ned's smiling daughter, Alice. (Jim Cunningham '71/Cornell Athletic Communications)

✦ MAN & SUPERMAN ✦

Ken Gilstein '70 was a student manager of the 1969–70 team. He says he still smiles when he thinks of that season. Some of his recollections:

My junior year, I was head manager of the lacrosse team. After the season, Ned Harkness came up to me and said, "Kenny, how'd you like to help out with the hockey team next year?" I could have fallen on the floor. Ned was really great to me—what a wonderful coach. I can still hear his voice during practice: *"Skate! Skate! Skate!"* He was a father figure. It was tough love sometimes, but there was a great heart behind that.

Before the first home game, they told me it was my job to take the sticks out to the bench. To do that, I had to carry them across the middle of the ice. So I put my arms out, palms up, and they loaded me up with all those sticks—twenty or thirty sticks. I got about halfway to the bench, and I slipped and fell. The sticks go high in the air and end up all over the place. I get a standing ovation from four thousand people. This was the highlight of my athletic career. And then the team comes out and they're asking me, "Hey, what was all that applause?" So I told them, and it was, "Welcome to the team, Kenny."

When we got to Lake Placid for the championship, it was a big factor that Dick Bertrand couldn't play. The lines had to be rearranged. Lots of adjustments had to be made, especially in the first game against Wisconsin. One thing I clearly remember about that game: when Wisconsin got the first goal to go ahead, all you could hear from their fans was "Twenty-seven and one! Twenty-seven and one!" Then Garth Ryan scored to tie it, and Bill Duthie got the go-ahead goal. That changed the whole complexion of the game. Bill was a good player, but I don't think he scored much during the season. It was a big turning point.

Going into the final game with Clarkson, the mood was much more relaxed. We had beaten them the week before. But in the third period, it was close and there were a couple of quick calls against us—and then Danny Lodboa decided he was going to be Superman.

Ned didn't tell the team he was leaving until after the NCAA championship game. But between the first and the second games, if I remember it right, he took the managers aside and said, "Well, I've got this offer from the Detroit Red Wings, and I'm not sure what I want to do." We all kind of looked at each other and said, "Uh-oh." Ned asked us not to say anything to the players and said he'd make an announcement once the season was over. We didn't want to see him leave, but we wanted the best for him—and he trusted us not to say anything.

That was a hell of a team, both talent-wise and personality-wise. They were a great bunch of guys, and they always treated me well—like I was one of the team, not just, "Oh, a stupid manager."

1970 NATIONAL CHAMPIONS

Won 29,   Lost 0
(Greatest Record in History of Collegiate Hockey)

Ivy League Champions   Eastern Champions

Seated: Bob Rule, Kevin Pettit, Steve Giuliani, Capt. Dick Bertrand, Capt. John Hughes, Capt.
Dan Lodboa, Garth Ryan, Ian Orr, Gordie Lowe, Brian Cropper.
Second Row: Coach Ned Harkness, Advisor Ellis Leonard, Jim Higgs, Bob Aitchison, Doug Ste-
wart, Bill Perras, Bill Duthie, Mark Davis, Ron Simpson, Larry Fullan, Brian
McCutcheon, Assistant Coach Rick Fullan, Trainer Alf Ekman.
Top Row: Assist. Manager Ken Gilstein, Ed Ambis, Dave Westner, Manager Steve Gorkin, Craig
Brush, Assist. Manager Artie Roth.

After the season, the official photo of the 1969–70 Cornell team honored them for posting the "Greatest Record in History of Collegiate Hockey."
Since then, no other Division I men's hockey team has matched the Big Red's undefeated, untied record. (Cornell Athletic Communications)

WISCONSIN 6, CORNELL 5 OT
BOSTON GARDEN, BOSTON, MASSACHUSETTS, MARCH 16, 1973

In the cavernous environs of the old Boston Garden, the Faithful began the countdown: "Ten . . . nine . . . eight . . . seven . . . six . . . five . . ." And then they fell silent.

It was the semifinal game of the 1973 NCAA Tournament, in Dick Bertrand's third year as Cornell's head coach. Soon after the celebrations for the 1970 NCAA championship died down, Ned Harkness had announced that he would be leaving Cornell to become head coach of the NHL's Detroit Red Wings. He wanted Bertrand to succeed him. It was an unusual idea, asking a just-graduated player to take over the team, even if Bertrand was older and more experienced than the other players.

Harkness thought Bertrand was the right choice, and he

wasn't a man who would take no for an answer. "Ned came after me," says Bertrand. "I had been interviewing with a lot of companies, but he just kept on me and kept on me. Finally I decided to take a shot at it." Bertrand says he talked it over with his returning teammates, wanting to be sure they would accept him as their coach. He also approached the incoming freshmen that Harkness had recruited, worried that some of them might not want to come to Cornell after the coaching change. In both cases, Bertrand got positive reinforcement.

Bertrand's first season behind the bench produced an impressive 22–5 record, although the Big Red lost in the ECAC semifinal to Clarkson. The next year they were 23–6, but the season ended with painful losses to Boston University in the 1972 ECAC and NCAA finals. The 1972–73 squad was again talented but played erratically, losing some games by one-sided scores but eventually advancing to the final of the ECAC

(*facing page*) The 1972–73 Big Red men's hockey team won the ECAC championship and advanced to the NCAA Tournament. (Courtesy of the Division of Rare and Manuscript Collections, Cornell University Library)

In his third season as the head coach, Dick Bertrand won the ECAC champi-onship and took the Big Red to the NCAA Tournament for the second year in a row. Pictured here with 1972–73 co-captains Bill Hanson (left) and Dave Street, Bertrand faced "Badger Bob" Johnson and his strong Wisconsin team in the national semifinal. (Cornell Athletic Communications)

Tournament, where they defeated Boston College 3–2 for Bertrand's first conference championship as head coach.

The Big Red moved on to the NCAA Tournament, which was still a four-team affair, matching the two top teams from the East, Cornell and Boston College, with the best from the West, Wisconsin and Denver. In the semifinal, the Big Red would face the Badgers. Head coach Bob Johnson undoubtedly had his 2–1 semifinal loss to Ned Harkness's 1970 champi-ons on his mind as the game started. And he couldn't have felt good when Cornell's Doug Marrett '74 netted a rebound only forty seconds into the game. The Big Red kept up the pressure on Wisconsin goalie Don Perkins throughout the period, and third-line forward Paul Perras '75 eventually cashed in, scoring a goal at 8:52 that made it 2–0.

Only thirty-one seconds into the second period, defenseman George Kuzmicz '74 blasted a slap shot past Perkins to put Cor-nell ahead by three goals. "Then Mike McGuire '73 hit from a steep angle on the right side at 4:39," Bill Howard '74 reported in the *Cornell Daily Sun*, "and the 70-piece Wisconsin band and 2,000 Wisconsin rooters realized that the end of the trail had about been reached for the Badgers."

Or maybe not. Kuzmicz was sent off for interference at 11:03, and Wisconsin got their first goal a minute later. The Badgers continued to forecheck and their offensive-zone pressure paid off at 18:28 when Cornell goalie Dave Elenbaas '73 was caught out of position and Dennis Olmstead netted a ten-footer. The period ended with Cornell up 4–2.

As the third period opened, the Big Red once again scored a quick goal: at forty seconds Bill Murray '74 put one past

George Kuzmicz, a junior in 1972–73, continued the tradition of outstanding Cornell defensemen. He would be named an All-American as a senior. His goal early in the second period gave the Big Red a 3–0 lead against Wisconsin. (Cornell Athletic Communications)

Mike McGuire's goal put Cornell ahead 4–0 and temporarily silenced more than two thousand Wisconsin fans in Boston Garden. The big lead would, unfortunately, prove to be short-lived. (Cornell Athletic Communications)

Goalie Dave Elenbaas says that his team lost focus late in the game, falling back defensively rather than continuing their forecheck: "We were trying to protect the lead, which is absolutely the wrong thing to do." (Cornell Athletic Communications)

Early in the overtime, center Don Ceci had a great opportunity on a two-on-none breakaway with linemate Paul Perras. His shot missed the net. (Cornell Athletic Communications)

With Cornell leading 5–4 and time running out, a pass went to Wisconsin's Dean Talafous (at far left). His quick shot eluded Dave Elenbaas (looking back in center photo), tying the score with only five seconds remaining and triggering a celebration by the Badgers. (Courtesy of University of Wisconsin Athletics)

Perkins to make it 5–2. Surely a three-goal lead in the third would be enough . . . wouldn't it?

Wisconsin answered that question with a goal shortly before the midperiod mark and then another with 3:12 remaining. Suddenly, it was a one-goal game. "I think we just fell back on our heels," says Elenbaas. "We were trying to protect the lead, which is absolutely the wrong thing to do. You've got to keep playing two-way hockey."

Cornell kept trying to push the puck out of their end as the clock wound down. Johnson pulled his goalie for an extra attacker, and the Wisconsin players swarmed Elenbaas. "John Taft hit the post with 15 seconds to play," wrote Howard in the *Sun*, "and as the Cornell fans ticked off the seconds, Stan Hinckley passed to [Dean] Talafous, who was three feet from the cage. The Cornell count stopped at five."

The score was tied. Overtime. Cornell came out strong and narrowly missed ending the game on several good scoring chances, including a two-on-none breakaway by Perras and linemate Don Ceci '74. As the final minute ticked away, it looked as if there would be another OT period. And then Talafous struck again, finding the net open on the left side and scoring the game winner with thirty-three seconds left. The Wisconsin fans were delirious.

The demoralized Big Red had one more game to play, as the NCAA format still called for a consolation contest. Despite outshooting Boston College by 47 to 29, Cornell lost 3–1. "I don't think our heads were in the game," says Elenbaas. "And I know we would not have felt any better if we had won that game."

Wisconsin went on to win the national title, defeating Denver 4–2 to give "Badger Bob" Johnson the first of his three NCAA championships. It had been a great season for Cornell, but the memory of those five seconds would linger.

Reggie Baker (left) was determined to have a women's hockey team at Cornell. With the help of Gail Murphy, one of her teachers at Lansing High School, she put the plans in motion before she even started classes. The player sitting next to her in this photo is goalie Amy Andersen. (Courtesy of Amy Andersen Kelsey)

CORNELL 3, BROWN 2
MEEHAN AUDITORIUM, PROVIDENCE, RHODE ISLAND, MARCH 6, 1976

Cornell women's ice hockey began with one determined student. In 1971, freshman Regina Baker knew that she wanted Cornell to have a team and took action to get one started. At the time, there were few women's teams at colleges in the United States, and among the Ivy League schools only Brown had established a program. Baker wanted Cornell to have the second Ivy women's team, and she recruited one of her teachers at Lansing High School, Gail Murphy, to help her even before she arrived on campus.

Cornell's athletics administration was reluctant at first—hockey was too dangerous for women, some believed—but they eventually approved the idea. There were no resources to speak of; equipment was borrowed or adapted from what men were using, and ice time at Lynah Rink cost $40 an hour. But Baker and Murphy stuck with it, and the Cornell club team played its first games in the 1971–72 school year. Their only intercollegiate contest was a 14–0 loss to McMaster University of Canada, but the program was moving forward.

In the next school year, the team was granted varsity status and Bill Duthie became the head coach. Duthie had played on the undefeated 1970 men's championship team, and he brought the right combination of knowledge and patience to the program. "Reggie Baker and Gail Murphy had a couple of guys who helped the first year," he says. "The next year, those two guys had graduated and left. John Hughes and I were down at the Fall Creek House one night, and the girls approached us about coaching them."

While some male players and coaches were skeptical about women playing the game—Ned Harkness was reportedly not in favor of it—Hughes is quick to praise the players that he coached. "Those women were pioneers," he says. "They played for all the right reasons. They dared to do something that wasn't

Bill Duthie, a member of the undefeated 1970 men's team, was named head coach of Cornell's first varsity women's ice hockey team for the 1972–73 season. Assisted by John Hughes, he would lead the team to its first Ivy League championship in 1976. (Cornell Athletic Communications)

thought of as what women normally did in those days. They were doing it because they wanted to learn new skills—and they were competitive."

Duthie's first varsity team played eight games against an assortment of U.S. and Canadian schools, winning four and losing four. They dropped two to the Brown team, which had been established in 1964, by 4–0 and 4–2 scores. The schedule expanded to ten games in 1973–74, and the Cornell women defeated Brown three times. The slate grew again the following season; the team posted a 12–2 record that included a victory over Princeton.

This was before Title IX, which gave equal status to women's athletics, and it was tough going. The players rode to their away games in vans, slept four to a room, and ate sandwiches. And some of their opponents were much more experienced. "I can remember going to a tournament with two teams from Canada," says Duthie. "Our kids weren't used to that level of hockey—and those Canadian kids knew how to intimidate you. One time Johnny Hughes was on the bench, and this one tough girl hit a kid on our team. Our kid whacked her in the back of the leg with her stick, and this other girl turned around and started chasing her. Our kid came right off the ice and hid in Johnny's coat."

The 1975–76 season was a landmark for Cornell and for women's hockey. An ever-growing number of potential opponents meant that Cornell could play a seventeen-game schedule—and for the first time there would be an Ivy League championship at stake. With the addition of a women's team at Yale, four Ivy schools were now competing. The first women's

The women's team did not have its own locker room, and players had to dress for practices in Lynah Rink's public-skating warming room. Much of their equipment was borrowed or adapted from what the men's team used, and their travel accommodations were less than luxurious. (Courtesy of Amy Andersen Kelsey)

The 1975–76 women's team played a seventeen-game schedule that included three other Ivy League schools. They posted a 12-5 record. (Courtesy of the *Cornellian*)

Coach Bill Duthie meeting with his players to discuss strategy. He was impressed with their determination, although many lacked basic skills. His patience and emphasis on fundamentals were crucial factors in the team's early success. (Cornell Athletic Communications)

Diana "Sunshine" Lorenz was one of the most experienced skaters on the team, having played for the Massport Jets in Boston before coming to Cornell. She scored all three Big Red goals in the championship game. (Cornell Athletic Communications)

IVY LEAGUE WOMEN'S HOCKEY TOURNAMENT

BROWN UNIVERSITY
Meehan Rink

Brown   **Yale**
Princeton   **Cornell**

March 5-6, 1976

The program for the first Ivy League women's hockey tournament, hosted by Brown University in March 1976, listed the four participating programs. They were among the first women's collegiate teams in the nation. (Courtesy of Brown University Athletics)

tournament was established, with Brown, Princeton, Yale, and Cornell meeting in Providence, Rhode Island, in March 1976.

There was little fanfare about the tournament, and attendance was sparse—mostly family members and friends. The *Cornell Daily Sun* had published a short preview, stating: "The icers are confident, having beaten Brown and Princeton in the regular season. However, they have never played Yale, which will probably prove to be their toughest opponent." Not exactly. In the tournament's opening game, the Big Red women demolished Yale 10–1. Star winger Cyndy Schlaepfer '78—who would be inducted into the Cornell Athletics Hall of Fame in 1985—scored seven goals. Her teammate Sunshine Lorenz '78 assisted on six of those goals and tallied two of her own. Schlaepfer is modest about her goal-scoring outburst. "Part of the reason we were scoring so many goals back then, in my opinion, is that the skaters were so much further ahead of the goalies," she says. "The attitude was, 'Who wants to play goal?' By the time I graduated, that had shifted. There were some really good goalies by then."

In the championship game, Cornell faced Brown, 4–0 victors over Princeton. The Pembroke Pandas—as the Brown team was known—scored first. The Cornell women struck back, on a goal by Lorenz with an assist by Schlaepfer. It appeared that the first period would end in a tie, but Lorenz scored again (with another assist from Schlaepfer) in the last second. Brown's coach and players argued that the period had ended before the puck crossed the line, but their protest was not upheld (and, needless to say, there was no video review in those days). "I can't say for sure," says Lorenz. "I do remember that it was very close to the buzzer. I was holding my breath—but the light went on. It counted." The Cornell women went into the locker room up 2–1.

The second period was scoreless. Cornell held its lead until the middle of the third period, when Brown forward Cathie Brady knotted the score at 2–2. Six minutes later, Lorenz struck again, off another feed from Schlaepfer. "Cyndy was great at digging the puck out of the corners," says Lorenz. "Strong—probably the strongest player on our team. She was very good at getting the puck to me in the slot."

Brown pressed the attack during the final minutes. "The Pandas went down fighting," reported the *Brown Daily Herald* the next day. "With just 20 seconds remaining to play Rita Harder's slap shot brought the crowd to its feet as the puck knifed [through] the Cornell defense and appeared to cross the goal line, though it was officially ruled to hit the pole."

No goal. Final score 3–2. The Cornell team skated away with the first Ivy League women's ice hockey championship, having outshot Brown 37 to 17 and showing the kind of puck control that Bill Duthie had learned from Ned Harkness. "What do I remember?" says Lorenz. "When my team headed to the locker room, I stayed behind. I wanted to savor the moment. I took a couple of victory laps around the empty arena, just to let the feeling sink in." It would be the first of six consecutive Ivy League titles won by Duthie's teams, which dominated the early years of Ivy women's competition and set a standard for the Cornell teams that followed.

✦ SUNSHINE'S STORY ✦

I skated on ponds for a long time before I joined a hockey program. Massachusetts didn't have any organized girls' hockey until I was in high school. My younger brothers had been playing on teams since they were five years old, but I didn't start until 1972. I skated for the Massport Jets out of East Boston.

I borrowed some equipment and wore white figure skates at my Jets tryout. Back then there was no such thing as girls' rules, so checking was allowed. I think their coach must have told his players to test my toughness, because every time the puck came near me, I was flattened. But I excelled in skating—that was my strength. After the tryout, the coach invited me to join the team. I said, "Dad, I need hockey skates." And he got me a pair of Bauer Supremes.

I chose Cornell because it had a women's hockey program. I wanted an Ivy League school, and I had done well in high school. In the summer of 1973, I traveled to Ithaca in a school bus with three or four of my Jets teammates. Dick Bertrand held a weeklong girls' hockey camp at Lynah. We were hosted in the homes of Cornell players and ate lunches in the dining halls. I fell in love with the campus. The next year, I applied early decision and got in.

Bill Duthie didn't really recruit in those days. Where would you recruit? There was no high school hockey for girls. So I came to campus, and in October they put the ice down. I still hadn't heard from Bill. I just showed up at the first tryout (everybody was a walk-on then), and Bill said to me, "We weren't even sure you came."

Everyone called me Sunshine. That was a nickname the Massport Jets gave me. At our practices in East Boston, I would wear an orange Philadelphia Flyers shirt and the girls teased me about it. "Oh, you're so bright we're going to have to wear sunglasses in the locker room." It was almost derogatory, but I decided to turn it around and adopt it.

For all four years I played at Cornell, we didn't have a locker room but kept our gear locked away beneath the Lynah Rink stairs opposite

Sunshine Lorenz was a strong player—and a strong advocate for her team. (Courtesy of Amy Andersen Kelsey)

the ticket window. After every practice and game we would shove our sweaty uniforms, wet skates, leather gloves, and soaked helmets back into our equipment bags until the next practice, when we would put our damp, cold gear back on—usually at 6 a.m. We used to joke that by the end of the season the bags would crawl out from under the stairs on their own.

For practices, we suited up in the public-skating warming room, on metal folding chairs. There were no showers. When we hosted visiting teams, we had to give up that room. I can't even remember where we changed, but I do remember that our "chalk talks" between periods were held in the Zamboni room. We would sit on wooden benches around the periphery of the room with our feet on pieces of rubber matting while the Zamboni cleared the ice.

Hardly anybody came to our games in the early years. My senior year, when I started dating my future husband, he would be almost the only person in the stands. He wrapped himself in a blanket because it was so cold in Lynah without any people.

We won a lot of games, but the *Daily Sun* didn't give us much ink. After we won the Ivy Tournament the first time and there was no mention of it in the *Sun*, I wrote an op-ed about the lack of coverage of women's sports. After our next game, they published an article on me. I guess they were thinking, "We'll show her—we'll put her picture in the paper."

I am proud to have been a part of those early years, when women's ice hockey was in its infancy. Maybe proud is not the right word—I am grateful. I have so many fond memories, not only of playing, but also of little things like singing songs together in the vans on the way to away games, and being hosted by local Cornell clubs. But what makes me feel honored is what has happened with one of my skates—now an ancient relic—that I gave to Coach Doug Derraugh '91 years ago. He uses it as a trophy—they call it the Cornell Cup—to motivate his players during intrasquad competitions held during daily practices. They compete throughout the week, and the winning squad gets to have their photo taken with my old skate, to hang in the locker room during the following week.

SUNSHINE LORENZ (DIANA LORENZ WEGGLER '78)

Brown goalie Kimberly Scala made thirty-four saves in the championship final. She called it "our best game of the season" and was bitterly disappointed in the loss. (Courtesy of Brown University Athletics)

In the third period, Sunshine Lorenz left the Brown defense behind as she moved in to score the game-winning goal. (Courtesy of Brown University Athletics)

Cornell goalies Amy Andersen (pictured) and Sandy Ward combined for fifteen saves in their team's victory over Brown. (Courtesy of Amy Andersen Kelsey)

CORNELL 6, PROVIDENCE 5 OT
LYNAH RINK, ITHACA, NEW YORK, MARCH 6, 1979

With Dick Bertrand behind the bench, Cornell was highly successful during the 1970s, consistently posting winning records and being in contention for an ECAC title nearly every year. But after winning the conference championship in 1973, they had a series of near misses, losing in the semifinal game for the next four years and then falling to Providence in the 1978 quarterfinal.

They also struggled against Boston University. After some initial victories over this old rival, they lost nine straight, including an infamous 9–0 thrashing at Lynah (later forfeited by BU for use of an ineligible player). The losing streak ended at

Lynah on January 6, 1979, when Cornell posted a 5–1 victory over the defending national champions and their outstanding goalie, Jim Craig—who would go on to "Miracle on Ice" fame the following year. The Big Red, riding on the emotion of that win, finished the regular season strong, winning eleven of their last thirteen games.

The only loss in the last month was to Providence—the same team that had bounced the Big Red from the ECAC Tournament the previous year. So, of course, when the 1979 quarterfinal matchups were announced, it was the Friars who would be coming to Lynah Rink. They had a potent offense and were coached by Lou Lamoriello, who would go on to a successful career as the coach and general manager of the NHL's New Jersey Devils.

Providence jumped out to a 2–0 lead in the first period as the Lynah Faithful looked on in stunned silence. There was an

(*facing page*) Radio announcer Roy Ives interviewed Robbie Gemmell after the game. During the third period, Ives had become so overwhelmed by the emotion in Lynah Rink that he was unable to speak—but he recovered his voice to call the end of the game. (Cornell Athletic Communications)

The 1978–79 team photo, showing one of the revised uniforms worn by the Big Red during the '70s. The design would be further changed in the '80s before returning to the "classic" Cornell look in 1987–88. (Cornell Athletic Communications)

unscheduled intermission in the second, when a bank of lights went out. "It was only for a couple of minutes," says Bertrand with a chuckle, "but Lou Lamoriello thought we did that on purpose." It didn't help. Play resumed—and when the buzzer sounded, the visitors held a 3–0 lead.

The game went from bad to worse when Providence's Tom Bauer scored at forty-six seconds of the third period. Cornell finally got the zero off its side of the scoreboard when John Stornik '79 took a pass from Brock Tredway '81 and beat Providence goalie Bill Milner—but then Bauer scored again, putting the Friars up 5–1.

With only sixteen minutes remaining, it looked hopeless. Cornell nonetheless pressed the attack, taking chances to keep the puck in the offensive zone. It paid off at 7:39, when Stornik deflected a shot from Lance Nethery '79 past Milner: 5–2. Two minutes later, Steve Hennessy '80 blasted a slap shot into the net: 5–3. Then, at 14:49, freshman John Olds '82 tallied for the Big Red: 5–4. Providence was back on their heels, trying desperately to clear their zone, and the Faithful were roaring. On the WHCU broadcast, announcer Roy Ives got so excited that he was momentarily unable to speak.

The game clock ran down to the last minute. The action was ferocious; the crowd noise deafening.

Lance Nethery describes what happened next: "With less than thirty seconds on the clock, there was a faceoff at the top of the circle in the Providence zone. Dick Bertrand had pulled the goalie, creating a six-on-five situation for us. The puck jumped forward off the faceoff, and one of their players pushed it past our defensemen, resulting in two players from Providence

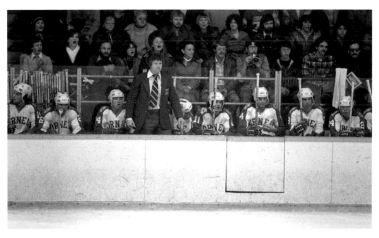

Head coach Dick Bertrand follows the action early in the playoff game against Providence. Things didn't look good for his team when the Friars jumped out to a 3–0 lead in the second period. (Cornell Athletic Communications)

Brock Tredway made the pass that led to the Big Red's first goal of the game, scored by John Stornik early in the third period. Tredway would finish his collegiate career with 113 total goals, which remains the Cornell record. (Cornell Athletic Communications)

skating in alone. The player with the puck, Randy Wilson, shot it toward our empty net. It hit the outside of the left post and went into corner. Steve Hennessy, one of our defensemen, retrieved the puck and passed it up to me. Not knowing how much time was left on the clock, I skated about five strides, and when I was between the red and blue lines, I decided to take a slap shot. The ice was pretty chewed up at the time, and as I hit the puck it was not lying perfectly flat. The puck dipped, or using a baseball term 'knuckleballed,' and went in between the legs of the Providence goalie. Tie game with thirteen seconds left."

In the overtime, Cornell controlled the puck and fired away at Milner, who had forty-three saves for the game. Four minutes into the extra period, Robbie Gemmell '79 grabbed a rebound and poked it past the struggling Providence goalie. Lynah exploded. "At the end of the game, the people just rolled out of the stands onto the ice," says Bertrand. "I'd never seen that before."

A wild celebration ensued. "The Cornell players, who were mobbing Gemmell at the east end of the rink, were in turn mobbed by onrushing fans," reported Mike Withiam in the *Ithaca Journal*. "Youngsters grabbed souvenir sticks; students raised high their posters, which had correctly predicted victory."

The game-tying goal was Nethery's last as a college hockey player. "Due to the unlikely circumstances that surrounded that goal," he says, "the game will be etched very clearly forever in my memory." Nethery's name is still in the Cornell record books as the team's all-time points leader, with 271. He also holds the career record for assists, with 180, and his teammate Brock Tredway holds the record for total goals, with 113. They were the most potent scoring combination in Big Red

Seconds after Providence's Randy Wilson missed an empty-net shot that would have iced the game, Lance Nethery's long-range blast tied the score. "As I hit the puck it was not lying perfectly flat," he recalls. "The puck dipped . . . and went in between the legs of the Providence goalie." (Cornell Athletic Communications)

hockey history.

Although Cornell lost its next game to New Hampshire in the ECAC semifinal, the contest against Providence firmly established this team's place in Cornell hockey lore. Its overtime victory was hailed by college hockey journalist and broadcaster Adam Wodon as "perhaps the most legendary game in the extraordinary history of Lynah Rink." No one who was there would disagree.

John Olds scored at 14:49 of the third period, pulling Cornell to within one goal after Providence had built what seemed to be an insurmountable 5–1 lead. (Cornell Athletic Communications)

Goalie Brian Hayward made twenty-three saves against Providence. His counterpart, Bill Milner, stopped forty-three pucks—but the last shot of the game eluded him. (Cornell Athletic Communications)

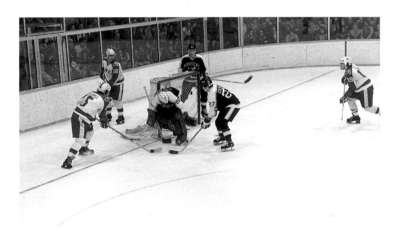

In the overtime, Cornell controlled the action. A shot by Brian Marrett went wide of the Providence goal, but Robbie Gemmell (at left) fired the rebound past the goalie for the game winner. (Cornell Athletic Communications)

As the Providence players looked on in disbelief, the Big Red team and the Lynah Faithful began their celebration of one of the most amazing comebacks in college hockey history. (Cornell Athletic Communications)

After the victory, the ecstatic Cornell fans swarmed over the boards to congratulate their heroes. "The people just rolled out of the stands onto the ice," says Dick Bertrand. "I'd never seen that before." (Cornell Athletic Communications)

A lengthy celebration capped Cornell's overtime victory, in what has been hailed as "perhaps the most legendary game" ever played at Lynah Rink. (Cornell Athletic Communications)

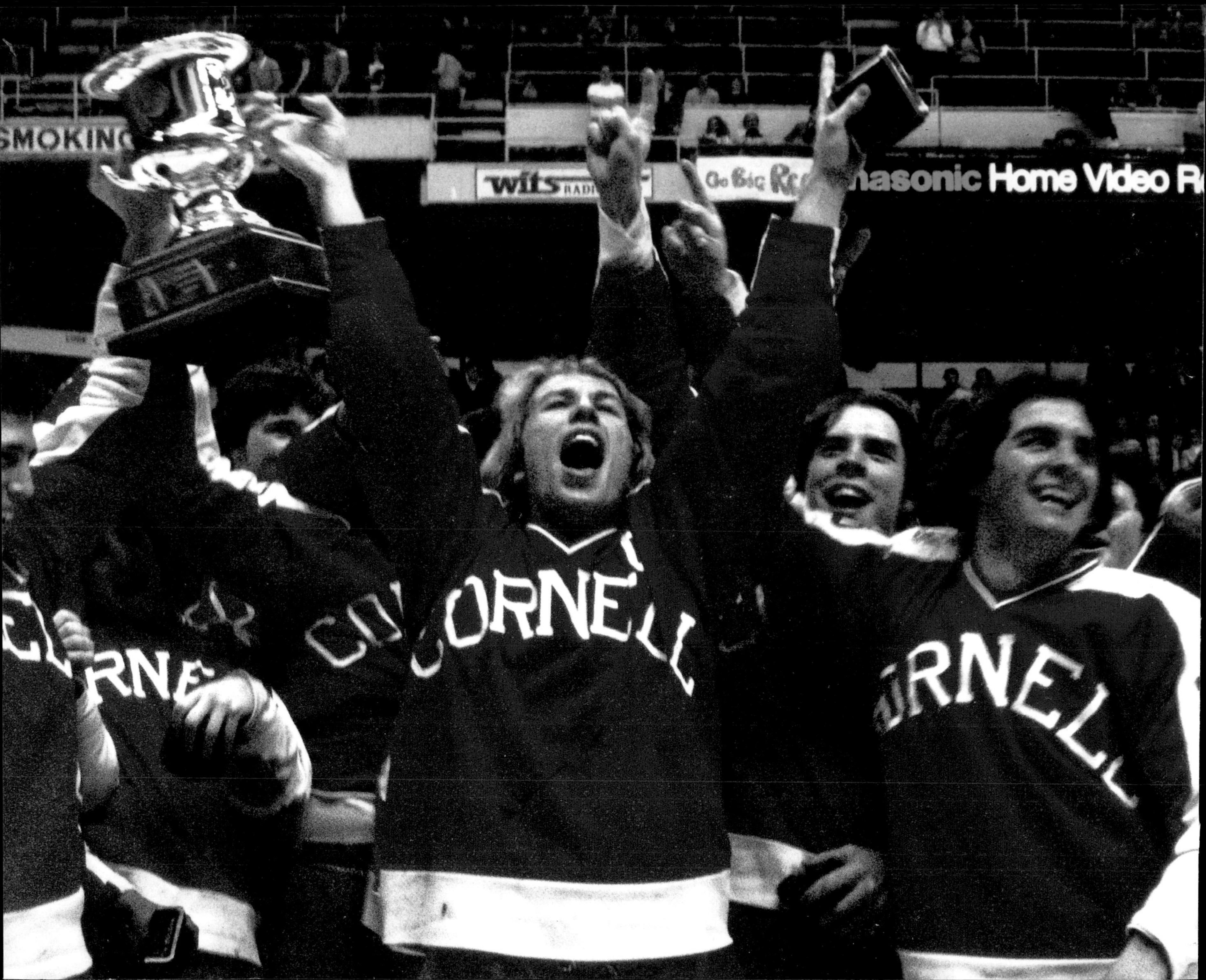
SMOKING
Go Big
Home Video

CORNELL 5, BOSTON COLLEGE 1
MCHUGH FORUM, CHESTNUT HILL, MASSACHUSETTS, MARCH 11, 1980

Dick Bertrand's team for the 1979–80 season featured perhaps the strongest pair of goaltenders in Cornell history: sophomore Brian Hayward '82 and freshman Darren Eliot '83, both of whom would go on to play in the NHL. Hayward figured to start most of the games, but Eliot says he arrived on campus believing that he would get some playing time. "I was seventeen years old and thought, *I'll just go and prove that I'm better*," he says. "We'll let the chips fall where they may."

The situation took an unexpected turn when Hayward contracted mononucleosis early in the school year and was unable to play, thrusting Eliot into the starting role. Hayward returned to the team in midseason but was not fully healthy and struggled

to regain his form. "With him not being himself and me being a freshman," says Eliot, "we had kind of an up-and-down, inconsistent season."

The Big Red started slowly, struggling to a 4–7 record. They lost 14–6 to Clarkson in mid-January, and then began to turn things around, winning four in a row. The inconsistency continued, however, and they needed to win their last two regular-season games for a chance to make it into the ECAC playoffs. After defeating Providence 5–2 at Lynah, only Boston University stood in their way. "That was a very strange game," recalls Eliot. "We were up 5–0, and then they started to come back. I had to go out of the game because my mask broke, and when I came back in it was tied." The game went to overtime, but a goal by Brian Marrett '80 finally won it.

The ECAC at that time had seventeen teams, divided into East, West, and Ivy divisions. Eight teams qualified for the

(facing page) Brock Tredway (center) leads his jubilant teammates in a "We're number one" salute as they hoist the ECAC championship trophy on March 15, 1980. (Courtesy of Dale Arrison Grossman '72)

Freshman goalie Darren Eliot was thrust into a starting role early in the 1979–80 season when Brian Hayward was out of action because of mononucleosis. Hayward later returned, but Eliot was chosen to start in the ECAC playoffs. (Cornell Athletic Communications)

Karl Habib was known for his tough, physical style. His hard check on Boston College captain Mike Ewanowski, who had to leave the game, was a key turning point in the quarterfinal playoff. (Cornell Athletic Communications)

playoffs: the three division champions and the five with the next highest winning percentages. "There was terrible pressure on the team in those days," says Roy Ives, who did radio play-by-play from 1972 to 1991. "They were expected to go to Boston every year. When the season started, the townies would start making plans for their trip to Boston."

With its 11–11 conference record, Cornell just barely qualified to make the playoffs, as the number 8 seed. They began in Chestnut Hill, on the home ice of number 1 seed Boston College for a one-game quarterfinal. "They were the top team in college hockey at the time, bar none," says Eliot. "We went into their building as the lowest seed, and they probably looked past us."

Big mistake. The Cornell players went into the game confident, feeling that their last two victories had given them momentum at just the right time. "We've all seen a single player get on a roll," says Brock Tredway. "When an entire team gets on a roll, that becomes scary—and that's what happened to us. You get to the point where losing is just not a concept you believe in."

Bertrand's team came out flying. "Cornell had BC running around in its own end much of the time by applying a strong forecheck, the strongest of any game this season," reported John Huenneke in the *Ithaca Journal*. "Cornell kept pressure on continuously for a full minute before [defenseman Joe] Gallant '82 rocketed a shot past Eagle goalie Doug Ellis just 3:10 into the game."

It was only one goal, and the BC players must have still believed that they could easily defeat this erratic opponent. Their fans cheered them on. And then, midway through the first period, a play silenced the crowd. "The turning point of that game was when Karl Habib '81 hit a BC player," recalls Bertrand. "Just

Dan Duffy capped the scoring against BC with a goal early in the third period that put Cornell ahead 5–1. The Big Red moved on to the ECAC championship round in the Boston Garden. (Cornell Athletic Communications)

Offensive sensation Brock Tredway gave the Big Red the lead for good with a goal near the end of the first period. Looking back on that game, he says, "When an entire team gets on a roll, that becomes scary—and that's what happened to us."(Cornell Athletic Communications)

Tredway's hard, accurate shot was a challenge to goalies throughout his Cornell career. He would go on to play professional hockey for four years. (Cornell Athletic Communications)

Darren Eliot continued the tradition of superb Big Red goaltending. He would be named an All-American in 1983, play in the NHL for five years, and become a sports broadcaster. (Cornell Athletic Communications)

Dick Bertrand's team faced Providence in the 1980 ECAC semifinal in the Boston Garden. They had defeated the Friars 5–2 at Lynah Rink only nine days before, but quickly fell behind their rivals from Rhode Island. (Cornell Athletic Communications)

Roy Kerling completed another amazing comeback against Providence, scoring the goal that put the Big Red ahead after they had fallen behind 5–2 early in the third period of the semifinal. (Cornell Athletic Communications)

In the ECAC final, goalie Darren Eliot made a save against Dartmouth's Dennis Murphy. (© *Cornell Daily Sun,* used by permission)

a really solid body check, right at center ice, that knocked the player flat on his back."

That player was BC's captain, Mike Ewanowski. Habib remembers the moment vividly: "He had the puck, head down, in the neutral zone, near their bench. I was able to come across and put a shoulder into his chest. I don't think he ever saw me. Down he went, and he didn't return to the game."

It was a clean hit—no penalty—and BC never recovered. Brock Tredway scored a second Cornell goal near the end of the first period, and the Big Red rolled from there, adding two goals in the second period and applying the coup de grâce when Habib's linemate Dan Duffy '82 scored just 1:19 into the third.

Eliot was stellar in goal, turning away BC shots repeatedly and making twenty-six saves in the game. The Eagles managed to score a meaningless goal with thirteen seconds remaining— Eliot's teammates were unhappy that he lost the shutout—but Cornell had pulled off what Huenneke called "one of the greatest upsets in ECAC Tournament history."

The underdogs from Ithaca advanced to the semifinal in Boston Garden, where they would once again face Providence, the number 2 seed. This game was much different from the one at BC. "It was a back-and-forth game," says Eliot, "with lots of good scoring chances for both sides."

Providence scored three times in the second period to take a 4–2 lead and added another goal only thirty-five seconds into the third—and then Cornell came roaring back. A minute after the fifth Providence tally, defenseman Dave Chiappini '83 scored on a long shot to make it 5–3. At 3:36, Jeff Baikie '83 launched another long slapper to make it 5–4. Then, on the power play,

As time wound down in the championship game, the Lynah Faithful began their celebration in Boston Garden. (© *Cornell Daily Sun,* used by permission)

As the scoreboard clock hit 0:00, the Big Red players surrounded Darren Eliot, who would be named the tournament's MVP, to congratulate him on his outstanding effort. A fan in the foreground signaled "We're number one!" (© *Cornell Daily Sun,* used by permission)

In the championship celebration in Ithaca, Darren Eliot shows President Frank Rhodes his ECAC Tournament MVP trophy. Behind him, co-captain Doug Berk holds the league championship trophy, Cornell's sixth. (Cornell Athletic Communications)

John Olds deflected a shot by Roy Kerling '81 into the goal to tie it with 7:08 left on the clock. As time wound down, Kerling completed the rally. He took a shot that was blocked by a Friar defenseman, but the puck came right back to him. He fired again, beating Providence goalie Scott Fiske stick-side with the game winner. Cornell moved on to face Dartmouth, the number 3 seed, for the ECAC championship. The Big Green had defeated Bertrand's team twice that year, winning 4–3 at Lynah and 8–3 in Hanover a week later. With strong play by goaltender Bob Gaudet—who would become the team's head coach in 1997—they had downed Clarkson 6–4 in the other semifinal.

Dartmouth had posted a 12–1–1 record in the fourteen games preceding the ECAC final and was an overwhelming favorite. It didn't matter. Midway through the first period, Tredway took a clearing pass from Eliot, deked around a Dartmouth defenseman, and put a shot over Gaudet's shoulder. Two more Cornell goals followed before the buzzer ended that period, and Dartmouth never recovered. The final score was 5–1, and Eliot was named the tournament's MVP. In the three games to decide the championship, the outstanding eighteen-year-old goalie had stopped ninety-one shots and posted a 2.33 goals-against average. He would play three more years at Cornell and be named a first-team All-American as a senior in 1983.

Once again, jubilant Cornell players hoisted the ECAC trophy and circled the ice. Afterward, the Lynah Faithful who had traveled to Boston took over the team's hotel. "It was just an absolute sea of red and white when we walked into the lobby," says Tredway. "You could not have packed another fan in there, and the band was there, too. It was an incredible, spontaneous outpouring of excitement. Everyone was so happy. It was just glorious."

(*facing page*) Dick Bertrand and his team saluted their supporters at Boston Garden after winning the ECAC championship game 5–1 over Dartmouth. It was Bertrand's second, and final, league title as head coach. (Courtesy of Dale Arrison Grossman '72)

The Cornell women's team had won five straight Ivy League championships and went into the 1980–81 season confident that they would take home another trophy. In the season-ending tournament, they blanked Dartmouth to advance to the final against Brown. (Cornell Athletic Communications)

CORNELL 4, BROWN 4 4OT
BRIGHT HOCKEY CENTER, CAMBRIDGE, MASSACHUSETTS, FEBRUARY 28, 1981

The Cornell women's team—winners of five straight Ivy League titles—entered the 1980–81 season with great expectations. And sure enough, they advanced to the championship game again, where they faced Brown, an opponent they were confident they could beat.

Under head coach Bill Duthie's watchful eye, the program had been getting stronger every year as it attracted talented recruits impressed by the team's success. The freshman class that had joined in 1979–80 was particularly deep, led by future stars Margaret "Digit" Degidio '83, Diane Dillon '83, and Liz Warren '83. In their sophomore year, they tackled an ambitious twenty-game schedule and started out well, with a win over Potsdam State. Then they stumbled a bit, losing four of the next five before a 14–0 victory over Québec-Trois Rivières in a tournament in Montreal. Building on the momentum from that big win, Duthie's squad won nine of eleven to close the regular season at 11–6–1.

The 1981 Ivy League Women's Ice Hockey Championship tournament was held at Harvard's Bright Hockey Center. The Cornell team, given a first-round bye, shut out Dartmouth 5–0 in the semifinal. They would face Brown—a team they had defeated 5–2 earlier in the year—for the championship. "We had that tradition of winning the Ivy League title, and that was something we took a lot of pride in," says Dillon, who had been the team's MVP in her first year. "That was, for us, the ultimate."

In the title game, Brown went ahead 1–0 on a goal at 3:26 of the first period, but Dillon quickly evened the score. She got another goal in the second to give her team the lead, but then the usually reliable Big Red defense faltered. The Brown women scored three straight goals to pull ahead, and their goalie, Jan Moody—who would be named MVP of the tournament—was making save after save. "Brown really wasn't a very good team," recalls Degidio, "but they had unbelievable goaltending."

With six minutes to go, Brown held a 4–2 lead. Then Degidio

Diane Dillon was an outstanding all-around player who had been the team MVP as a freshman. In the championship game, she scored the first two goals for the Big Red. (Jon Crispin/Cornell Athletic Communications)

Margaret Degidio—better known as "Digit"—scored an unassisted goal in the third period to pull her team within one goal. Another Cornell tally, by Brenda Condon, tied the score 4–4, which is where it remained at the end of regulation time. (Cornell Athletic Communications)

Cornell goalie Sarah Mott made thirty-two saves against Brown in the Ivy League championship game. Her Brown counterpart, Jan Moody, had thirty-nine saves and was named MVP of the tournament. (Cornell Athletic Communications)

stole the puck and broke into the offensive zone, scoring an unassisted goal that pulled her team within one. Things looked bad when Brown went on the power play, but a shorthanded goal by Brenda Condon '81 at 18:03 knotted the score. Cornell goalie Sarah Mott '81 refused to allow anything get past her after that, and the buzzer sounded with the score deadlocked at 4–4.

Neither team scored in the first ten-minute overtime period. Or in the second. Or in the third. The sound of the coaches shouting instructions echoed through the building, and the players struggled to keep their heavy legs moving. Excitement turned to exhaustion. "We were so amped up at first, but it went on and on and on," says Dillon. "It was hard to keep focused. Everybody wanted to be the hero, and then that started to turn for some of the players—they were afraid to be the goat. I was a captain, so I kept trying to rally the troops."

Bill Duthie and Brown coach Steve Shea met before the start of the fourth overtime period. If neither team scored, they agreed, they would end the game and finish as co-champions. And that's what happened.

It was Duthie's last Ivy League women's championship—he would step down after three more seasons with a career record of 135–85–5—and certainly his most unusual. Sharing the title was less than satisfying for his players. "We were *disgusted*," says Degidio, who was named the Ivy League Player of the Year for that season. "We were disgusted because they wouldn't let us finish the game. As an athlete, I felt cheated. There was some thought, I guess, that women couldn't handle it. It was ridiculous."

Dillon concurs: "It gives you an idea of where women's sports were at the time. They would never do anything like that today."

Ironically, perhaps, Degidio—known as Digit Murphy by then—would later become head coach of the Brown women's team, where she would serve for twenty-two years and record 318 victories. But she says it still bothers her when she sees the photograph of the Cornell and Brown women's teams together as 1981 Ivy League co-champions. "That picture haunts me to this day," she says. "There was no question in my mind that we were going to win that game."

The score remained deadlocked after four ten-minute overtime periods, so the head coaches agreed to end the game and name the teams co-champions. At the trophy presentation, the Brown players appeared to be happier with that result than the Cornell players—who were "disgusted," according to Margaret Degidio. (Courtesy of Brown University Athletics)

As a freshman, Joe Nieuwendyk had electrified the Lynah Faithful with his puck-handling skill and scoring prowess. He was honored as the ECAC Rookie of the Year. In his sophomore season, he was even better, scoring forty-two points and being named an All-American. (Cornell Athletic Communications)

CORNELL 3, CLARKSON 2 OT
BOSTON GARDEN, BOSTON, MASSACHUSETTS, MARCH 15, 1986

After leading his team to the ECAC championship in 1980, Dick Bertrand remained the head coach for two more years. In 1980–81, the Big Red had a strong season, finishing first in the ECAC's Ivy Region and advancing once again to the title game; they lost 8–4 to Providence and finished at 19–11–1. The following year, despite brilliant play by All-American goaltender Brian Hayward, the team failed to make the playoffs. Its final record was 12–13–1.

Believing it was time for a change, Bertrand stepped down as the head coach. His assistant, Lou Reycroft, was named to succeed him. Reycroft, who had been a goaltender at Brown, would coach the Big Red for five years. In his first two seasons, the team posted records of 13–10–3 and 11–15 and failed to make the playoffs. In 1984–85, led by junior defenseman Mike Schafer '86 and high-scoring freshman Joe Nieuwendyk '88, Reycroft's team turned the corner, advancing to the ECAC

semifinal against RPI. They lost that game 5–1, but bounced back to win the consolation 5–3 over Clarkson and finish at 18–10–2. It set the stage for their title run the next year.

As a senior, Schafer was a tri-captain, wearing the C along with classmates Duanne Moeser '86 and Peter Natyshak '86. That team quickly earned the nickname "Cardiac Kids," going to overtime in four of their first six games (wining two and tying two). The pattern continued throughout the year, and by the time they had gotten past Vermont in the first round of the ECAC playoffs, they had endured ten extra-time games, losing only two.

It was good preparation for the league championship round, once again held in the aging but beloved confines of Boston Garden. Cornell faced Yale in the semifinal. It was their fourth meeting of the year; the teams had split their regular-season contests and also met in a tournament in British Columbia, where Cornell won 5–3.

The 1985–86 Cornell team was led by senior tri-captains Mike Schafer, Duanne Moeser, and Pete Natyshak. In the team photo, Schafer is in the center of the front row; sophomore center Joe Nieuwendyk is standing right behind him. (Cornell Athletic Communications)

Reycroft's squad was confident. "We knew we had a good team, and we knew we had a good goalie," says Nieuwendyk. "Doug Dadswell '88 gave us a chance to win every night. He was an All-American. And in college hockey, if you can get on a roll in those one-game playoffs, you can go far."

Yale scored first, getting a power-play goal at 7:23 of the first period after Dadswell was penalized for interference. The Bull-dogs dominated play in the early part of the game, outshooting the Big Red 18–9 in the first twenty minutes—but Dadswell, who led the nation in save percentage that year, kept turning away scoring chances.

Two freshmen put Cornell ahead in the second period. Defenseman Alan Tigert '89 picked a good time to score the first goal of his Cornell career when he connected on a shot from the

After Dick Bertrand stepped down in 1982, Lou Reycroft was named head coach of the Big Red. Reycroft had been a goaltender at Brown and an assistant coach at RPI before coming to Cornell to serve as Bertrand's assistant for four years. (Jon Crispin/Cornell Athletic Communications)

As a player, defenseman Mike Schafer was known for his physical style—and for his savvy on the ice. His heads-up deflection of a Clarkson pass in the 1986 ECAC championship game led to the game-winning goal. (Cornell Athletic Communications)

Mike Schafer was not afraid to get in the face of an opposing player. (Cornell Athletic Communications)

blue line at 3:57. Four minutes later, forward Chris Grenier '89 knocked in a rebound of a Natyshak shot to make it 2–1. The lead didn't last long. At 10:01, with the teams skating four-on-four, Yale tied it up.

"The Cornell netminder stepped into the spotlight at that point," wrote Tom Fleischman of the *Ithaca Journal*. In the third period, Yale put eighteen shots on goal but failed to get one past Dadswell. Cornell also came up empty, so the game went to overtime. Yale continued to pour it on, outshooting Cornell 6–3—but the score remained tied.

"During the first overtime, they were really putting pressure on us," says Reycroft. "There's a faceoff in our end, and Mike Schafer comes to the bench and tells me that Doug is asking for a time-out. I said to Mike, 'Tell you what—just stay here at the bench. I don't know if I want to use the time-out now. We might want it later. Stay right here and talk to me. We'll make the referee come over.' So the referee, Ken McKinnon, came over, and I asked him a fake question. I said, 'We're in overtime, and we didn't use our time-out in regulation. Do I get a second one in overtime?' We're buying time, to get Dadswell some rest."

It paid off. Neither team scored, and the game went to another overtime. "Dadswell continued to dazzle in the second extra period," wrote Fleischman, "which started out with the Red's Joe Nieuwendyk in the penalty box." Cornell's offensive star had taken what Reycroft termed an "uncharacteristic" high-sticking penalty late in the first overtime.

"I remember getting that penalty and praying they wouldn't score," says Nieuwendyk. "When I came out of the box, I had a lot of speed, a lot of energy, and I was able to come around the net and make a play to Moeser. And he one-timed it, top shelf."

Nieuwendyk was falling as he reached out to make the pass, but the puck went right to Moeser's stick—and into the goal. "After the game," Reycroft recalls, "Duanne said to me that he had had a couple of good chances to score, and he had made up his mind that if he got one more chance, he was going to go up top on him. And that's exactly what he did."

The Cornell goalie made fifty-seven saves, eliciting chants of "Dads-well! Dads-well!" from the large red-clad contingent in the crowd and frustrating Yale coach Tim Taylor. "We simply couldn't get the puck past Dadswell," he said after the game. "He was sensational." Exhausted but elated, the Cornell players advanced to the final against a familiar opponent: Clarkson, upset winners over regular-season ECAC champions Harvard in the other semifinal game.

In their regular-season meetings, the teams had tied 3–3 early in the season at Lynah and Cornell had prevailed 4–2 in a February game at Walker Arena in Potsdam. They knew each other well, and the game was a taut, back-and-forth contest.

Cornell jumped out to a 1–0 lead in the first period on a goal by Pete Marcov '87. Dave Hunter '86 increased the lead at 3:45 of the second when he deflected a Schafer drive past Clarkson goalie Jamie Falle. The Golden Knights battled back, getting a five-on-three score at 12:13 and then tying the score on a power-play goal with only one second left in the period.

But was there still time on the clock? "Earlier in the period, a play ended but the clock operator didn't hear the whistle," says Reycroft. "So some time ran off the clock. They brought it to the attention of the referee, Pierre Belanger. Kind of quickly

Sophomore goalie Doug Dadswell made fifty-seven saves against Yale in the semifinal and thirty-one more in the championship game versus Clarkson, as the Lynah Faithful chanted his name. He was named MVP of the 1986 ECAC Tournament. (Cornell Athletic Communications)

In the ECAC semifinal against Yale at Boston Garden, Joe Nieuwendyk came flying out of the penalty box to make the play that led to the game-winning goal. (Tim McKinney/Cornell Athletic Communications)

Joe Nieuwendyk says that the bond he feels with his Cornell hockey teammates will "last forever." (Tim McKinney/Cornell Athletic Communications)

Nieuwendyk must have felt comfortable in the all-red uniforms of the NHL's Calgary Flames, one of the three teams he played on that won the Stanley Cup. (O-Pee-Chee/Hockey Hall of Fame, used by permission)

Duanne Moeser's shot won the semifinal at 1:14 of the second overtime. Lou Reycroft recalled the moment: "Duanne had made up his mind that if he got one more chance, he was going to go up top on [the Yale goalie]. And that's exactly what he did." (Cornell Athletic Communications)

and very arbitrarily, he put time back on the clock—and it was about ten more seconds than had run off. I sent somebody over to tell Belanger that, but he didn't want to hear it. And then Clarkson scores a goal with a second to go. So that decision about extra time resulted in it being a tie game, rather than us having a one-goal lead going into the third."

Questionable or not, the deadlock held up throughout the third period, although it looked as if Cornell had won it at 11:42 when Dave Crombeen '88 scored from the slot. Belanger waved off the goal, saying that Natyshak had made a hand pass to get the puck to Crombeen. So Cornell was once again going to overtime—with the ECAC championship and a trip to the NCAA Tournament on the line.

Things looked bad early in the OT, when Nieuwendyk was once again sent off for high-sticking. But the penalty killers were up to the job, diving in front of Clarkson shots and clearing the puck to maintain the tie. The teams battled up and down the ice, fighting fatigue and looking for scoring opportunities. And then, eight minutes into the extra period, Clarkson made a fatal mistake.

"One of their players made a pass coming out of their zone," says Reycroft, "and Mike Schafer read it." Schafer says that he was just trying to slow Clarkson's rush: "The puck came up the middle. I stepped up, looking for a hit—but then one of their guys made a bad pass. I was able to pick it off and bump it down the boards to Natyshak."

Natyshak sent the puck cross-ice to Chris Grenier, who was streaking down the middle. "It was a two-on-one," says Grenier. "Dave Crombeen was on my left. It seemed like a perfect opportunity to screen the goaltender, so I cut a little to the left. Falle was moving across, assuming that a pass was going to go to Crombeen, but I got a shot away. I caught him leaning to his right, and the puck went to the glove side high. I got tangled up with their player, the defender, but I was on cloud nine when I heard the crowd roar. Schafer grabbed me and hugged me. We fell down and the whole team jumped on top of us."

Doug Dadswell, who made thirty-one saves against Clarkson for a total of eighty-eight in the two games, was named the MVP of the tournament. He was presented the trophy by that year's tournament director, Cornell AD Laing Kennedy—the star goalie of the Big Red's early-'60s team. It would be Dadswell's last game for Cornell, as he signed a pro contract soon after the championship celebration.

Cornell advanced to the NCAA Tournament as the number 4 seed in the West Regional. At that time, it was an eight-team affair; the first round was a two-game series with the winner determined by total goals. The Big Red faced Denver, the number 1 seed—and almost pulled off another stunning upset. After losing 4–2 in the first game, they came back to take the second 4–3. "One of our defensemen, Andy Craig '87, had a shot in the final seconds of that game," recalls Grenier. "It was just a foot wide of the net." Lou Reycroft's finest team finished 21–7–4 and brought home the trophy for Cornell's seventh ECAC championship.

Freshman forward Chris Grenier made key plays in the ECAC Tournament. In the semifinal, his second-period goal gave Cornell the lead against Yale. The next night, he would score the deciding goal against Clarkson at 8:26 of the overtime, winning Cornell its seventh ECAC championship. (Cornell Athletic Communications)

CORNELL 6, HARVARD 2 & CORNELL 4, HARVARD 2

LYNAH RINK, ITHACA, NEW YORK, MARCH 2 & 3, 1990

After Boston University left the ECAC to join Hockey East in 1983, the intensity of that old rivalry diminished. In the new, smaller ECAC, Harvard emerged as a more important opponent, especially since both the Ivy League and ECAC titles were on the line in games against the Crimson. There was just one problem: Harvard kept winning the games.

For the 1987–88 season, Brian McCutcheon had returned to Ithaca as Cornell's new head coach. One of the stars of the undefeated 1970 NCAA champions and a captain of Dick Bertrand's team the next year, McCutcheon had played professionally for seven years—including thirty-seven games with the NHL's Detroit Red Wings—before moving on to coaching

at Elmira College. His Cornell teams had good initial success, posting 19–9 and 16–13–1 records in his first two years. His 1989–90 team started slowly and won only two of its first nine games, but then they took nine of the next ten on the way to a 14–9–3 record at the end of the regular season.

But Harvard continued to be a nemesis. Between 1985 and 1990, the Big Red had dropped eleven straight games to their rivals from Cambridge, including all seven since McCutcheon had taken over. Under legendary head coach Bill Cleary, Harvard had won the 1989 NCAA championship, and they remained a potent if less consistent team the following season—and they were Cornell's opponent in the first round of the ECAC Tournament.

As the number 3 seed, the Big Red would face the number 6 Crimson in the friendly confines of Lynah Rink for a quarterfinal series. "Coming off their national championship, Harvard

---

Ross Lemon (23) celebrated after scoring the power-play goal that put the Big Red ahead 6–2 late in the first game. (© *Cornell Daily Sun*, used by permission)

The Cornell players congratulated Doug Derraugh after he scored on Harvard goalie Allain Roy to put the Big Red ahead 1–0 early in the second game. They would never relinquish the lead. (© *Cornell Daily Sun*, used by permission)

Cornell's Phil Nobel celebrated with a cigar after his team's victory in game two clinched the playoff series for the Big Red. (© *Cornell Daily Sun*, used by permission)

The 1989–90 Big Red team, led by captain Casey Jones, was determined to reverse the tide against Harvard, which had won eleven straight games over Cornell and was the reigning NCAA champion. (Cornell Athletic Communications)

In the first game of the ECAC quarterfinals at Lynah Rink, freshman forward Kent Manderville scored late in the first period to put Cornell ahead 2–1. Manderville would be named the ECAC Rookie of the Year for 1989–90. (© *Cornell Daily Sun*, used by permission)

Brian McCutcheon, who had played on the first line of the undefeated 1970 team, returned to Cornell as the head coach for the 1987–88 season. Standing to his left in this photo is assistant coach Mike Schafer, who would become the head coach himself in 1995. (Cornell Athletic Communications)

Goalie Jim Crozier made fifty-one saves in the two victories over the Crimson. After the second game, he was praised by Harvard coach Bill Cleary, who said, "He came up big." (Cornell Athletic Communications)

had that swagger," says Jim Crozier '91, the Cornell goalie. "And certainly Coach Cleary had a swagger about him. He probably felt that he was going to come out of Ithaca with a win."

On the first day of the playoffs, a *Daily Sun* editorial titled "Harvard Who?" urged the Cornell players to look beyond the losing streak: "The games tonight and tomorrow are very important for Cornell's hockey team, but the focus should be on the playoffs, not on the identity of the opposing team. Harvard just doesn't deserve that kind of special recognition."

The message resonated with the Cornell players. "We were aware of our record against them, but it didn't psych us out at all," says Ross Lemon '90, the team's leading goal scorer. "We figured that two wins that weekend would cure what had ailed us."

For the opening faceoff, the line centered by team captain Casey Jones '90 faced Harvard's top line. "I remember looking over at Alex Nikolic '92, who was a pretty physical player," says Jones. "He was matched up with C. J. Young, a skilled kid. Alex told him, 'I'm in charge of keeping you off the [score]board,' and he had him so flustered that C. J. was about fifteen feet off the line. Looking at that, I felt really good about how things were going to go."

Although they gave up an early goal, the Cornell players were unfazed. They were determined to end the losing streak. A Big Red power play tied the score midway through the first period, on a rebound put-back by center Ryan Hughes '93. Then, with twenty-one seconds remaining in the period, Kent Manderville '93 blew past the Harvard defense and beat goalie Chuckie Hughes to put Cornell ahead 2–1.

After Harvard had tied the score in the second period of the first game, Doug Derraugh fought off a check in front of the net and scored to put the Big Red ahead 3–2. It would prove to be the game-winning goal. (© *Cornell Daily Sun*, used by permission)

In his four years at Cornell, Casey Jones scored 112 points. After graduating, he served as an assistant coach under McCutcheon before moving on to similar positions at Clarkson and Ohio State. He returned as Cornell's associate head coach in 2008 and was named the head coach at Clarkson in 2011. (© *Cornell Daily Sun*, used by permission)

Kent Manderville had a stellar two-year career at Cornell before moving on to play with the Canadian National Team and six NHL squads. (Cornell Athletic Communications)

The Crimson made it 2–2 at 4:21 of the second period, but their second goal would be their last. An outstanding winger named Doug Derraugh '91 put Cornell ahead 3–2 less than two minutes later. "I had to come out of the corner and got in a bit of a scuffle with a defenseman," says Derraugh. "I managed to get a stick on the puck and took a shot. After I scored, my face mask was pushed up over my head and my helmet was all twisted. So hard work in front of the net paid off on that one."

Then Cornell's fourth line—Jason Vogel '93, Jim Goerz '90, and Phil Nobel '92—got into the act. Nobel dug the puck out of the corner and fed it to Vogel for the tally that made it 4–2. And just before the period ended, Derraugh scored again to push the lead to 5–2.

Harvard was out of gas and couldn't mount a rally in the final period, despite two early penalties against Cornell. With seven minutes remaining, Lemon put the game away, taking a long pass from Jones and beating the beleaguered Harvard goalie to make the final score 6–2. "My goal was a slap shot that I never dreamed was going to go in," says Lemon. "I was just trying to get it on net, but it went top shelf. Everything went our way that night."

With a minute left, the Lynah Faithful rose to their feet and gave the team a sustained standing ovation. "The fans were phenomenal," says Crozier. "That's one of the special memories that I have when I look back at my career at Cornell, the fans at Lynah that weekend." It was a big win for the Big Red—but they needed another one.

On Saturday night, Cleary started Allain Roy in goal instead of Hughes. McCutcheon stuck with Crozier, who had made twenty-six saves the night before. He came up big again.

The Big Red started out where they had finished the night before, dominating early play and scoring two goals in 2:02. Derraugh got the first one, grabbing a loose puck in the right circle and sending it past Roy. Then Lemon put Cornell up 2–0 by one-timing a pass from Jones into the Harvard net. "Doug's a pretty reserved guy, but he was so fired up after that first goal that the whole bench noticed it," says Lemon. "Then I got the second one, and I've never been reserved—that was about as crazy as I got after a goal. You could see that everyone was thinking, *There's no way we're losing this now.* We were just so focused."

Harvard got a goal at 7:59 to make the score 2–1 at the end of the first period. Then, perhaps because they were overcompensating—or as the Faithful would say, "Frustrated!"—the Crimson were hit with five penalties in the second period. Cornell cashed in, getting power-play goals from Hughes and Trent Andison '91 to push the score to 4–1. Harvard got one more goal in the third period, but the Big Red defense held firm as time ran down, repeatedly clearing the puck from the defensive zone.

Crimson star Ted Donato, who would become his alma mater's head coach in 2004, capped his team's lost weekend by getting hit with a ten-minute misconduct penalty in the final minute. As the buzzer sounded, the Faithful spilled over the boards to salute their heroes. "The fans just poured on the ice," says Lemon. "As seniors, we did not want our last game at Lynah Rink to be a loss to Harvard. It just wasn't going to end that way."

Crozier made twenty-five saves, and after the game Cleary expressed his admiration for the junior goaltender. "He played very well," he said. "We had some great opportunities, and he came up big. You've got to admire the boy—he did a wonderful job." It was Cleary's final game as Harvard's head hockey coach, as he moved on to become the university's athletic director the next year.

Cornell advanced to the ECAC semifinal in Boston Garden but fell to RPI to finish the season at 16–10–3. Even so, the two victories over Harvard in the playoff games at Lynah were a key moment in McCutcheon's tenure. "That series was important," he says. "We felt that with our recruiting, with the players that we'd brought in, we were turning the corner as far as being a national contender again. Harvard had won the national championship, and they were one of those teams you were looking at to measure yourself against. To be able to beat them two nights in a row was very exciting."

Kent Manderville scored many big goals for the Big Red—but none were more timely than the one he tallied against Michigan late in the first game of the 1991 NCAA Tournament. (© *Cornell Daily Sun*, used by permission)

CORNELL 5, MICHIGAN 4 OT
YOST ICE ARENA, ANN ARBOR, MICHIGAN, MARCH 15, 1991

As the number 6 seed from the East in the 1991 NCAA Tournament, the Big Red traveled to face a powerhouse Michigan team (32–7–3) in a best-of-three series. The Wolverines' home rink, Yost Ice Arena, held more than six thousand fans—and a very large band. "I think they brought the entire hundred-piece brass band," says head coach Brian McCutcheon. "Before the game, I was sitting up in the rafters listening to this band and getting a headache."

In the first game, Michigan came out flying, and winger Dan Stiver got a shot past Cornell goalie Jim Crozier before two minutes had elapsed. The rest of the period featured plenty of hard hits but no more scoring until Big Red defenseman Bruce Frauley '91 tied it with 1:13 left on the clock.

Cornell took the lead in the second when Doug Derraugh cashed in a pass from Ryan Hughes, putting it between the legs of Michigan goalie Steve Shields to make it 2–1. It took the Wolverines all of ten seconds to erase the lead, when a Cornell turnover after the faceoff resulted in a two-on-one. Undaunted, the Big Red kept battling their favored opponent on even terms until Kent Manderville was able to collect a loose puck, break into the offensive zone, and beat Shields with a backhand. Once again, Michigan fought back to tie it just before the second period ended.

❊ ❊ ❊

Brian McCutcheon's team had started strong that year, with six wins and two ties in their first ten games, but they had problems with consistency, never winning more than three games in a row. They lost three of four at the end of the regular season to finish in second place in the conference, one point behind Clarkson, and faced Colgate in a best-of-three ECAC quarterfinal series

Despite losing a "heartbreaker" to St. Lawrence in the ECAC semifinal playoff game, Cornell was selected for the 1991 NCAA Tournament. The team traveled to Yost Ice Arena in Ann Arbor to face a strong University of Michigan team—and more than six thousand vociferous Wolverine fans. (Cornell Athletic Communications)

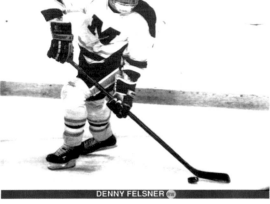

DENNY FELSNER RW

HOBEY BAKER FINALIST/ALL-AMERICAN CANDIDATE

CORNELL
NCAA HOCKEY CHAMPIONSHIPS - FIRST ROUND
March 15-17, 1991 • Yost Ice Arena • Ann Arbor, MI • Official Program $2.00

The program for the NCAA playoff series featured Wolverine star Denny Felsner. He had thirty-eight goals and thirty-one assists in the regular season, but the Big Red defense shut him down in the first game. (Scan courtesy of Arthur Mintz)

The Big Red were led by co-captains Doug Derraugh (left) and Dan Ratushny. A powerful defenseman, Ratushny was named an All-American for the 1990–91 season before leaving school to play for the Canadian Olympic team. Derraugh would finish the season with sixty-six points, for a total of 153 in his Cornell career. After playing professionally in Europe, he returned to Cornell in 2005 as head coach of the women's team. (Cornell Athletic Communications)

Jim Crozier gave up a goal to Michigan early in the game, but on this play he stopped a scoring effort by David Roberts. (© *Cornell Daily Sun*, used by permission)

A pass from Ryan Hughes (pictured) to Doug Derraugh early in the second period gave Cornell a 2–1 lead. (Cornell Athletic Communications)

Cavernous Yost Ice Arena was filled with vociferous Michigan fans for the best-of-three playoff series. (© *Cornell Daily Sun*, used by permission)

at Lynah Rink. The teams had played two close games that year, a 4–4 tie in November and a 3–2 Cornell victory in January, so what happened in the playoff was surprising: the Big Red won the first game 10–3 and the second 8–1.

Cornell moved on to the ECAC semifinal at Boston Garden, where they faced St. Lawrence, a team they had beaten twice that season. But they fell just short, losing a "heartbreaker," as McCutcheon put it, 4–3 in overtime. Their season appeared to be over—but then they were picked as one of the twelve teams in the NCAA Tournament that year, six each from the East and West, playing two rounds of best-of-three to pare down the field to the four finalists. The selection committee apparently felt that Cornell's strength of schedule had earned it a spot, and the way they were playing against Michigan showed the committee was right.

In the third period at Yost, Cornell had two early power plays but failed to score. When the tables were turned, Michigan immediately took advantage of the opportunity, getting a goal only eight seconds into a power play to go ahead 4–3. Sitting on the lead as their fans howled, Michigan kept clearing the puck. Cornell kept pushing it back in. Ryan Hughes got off a good slap shot, but it hit the post. Michigan cleared again. With thirty-one seconds left, McCutcheon called a time-out to review extra-attacker strategy that the team had practiced. On the ensuing faceoff, the Big Red got possession of the puck and goalie Crozier headed to the bench.

"Cornell won a faceoff in the Michigan end with eight seconds left," reported Tom Fleischman in the *Ithaca Journal*, "but CU defenseman Dan Ratushny '92 fell to the ice with six to go

Kent Manderville was inspired by the Lynah Faithful who had made the journey to Michigan: "You could hear those pockets of people in the stands." (Cornell Athletic Communications)

With only two seconds remaining in regulation, Joe Dragon got the puck to Kent Manderville in front of the Michigan goal. His quick shot beat goalie Steve Shields to tie the game—and silence the Michigan fans. (© *Cornell Daily Sun*, used by permission)

As the stunned Wolverine fans looked on, the Cornell players celebrated after Trent Andison's shot won the game in overtime. (© *Cornell Daily Sun*, used by permission)

The scoreboard sums it up: Cornell 5, Michigan 4. (© *Cornell Daily Sun*, used by permission)

as he attempted to control the puck at the right point. Derraugh managed to fire the puck around the boards to center Joe Dragon '92, who spotted Manderville in front of the net."

The Michigan fans were counting down the final seconds. They got to three—and stopped. Dragon had passed to Manderville, who one-timed the puck into the upper left corner of the goal. "Shields was a really big goalie," says Manderville, "and I just wanted to get the puck up. It wasn't even a hard shot. When it went in, there was dead silence—except for a few Cornell fans. You could hear those pockets of people in the stands. And then I was swarmed by my teammates."

With two seconds left, the score was 4–4. The game went into overtime. The Michigan players, stunned by what had just happened, never got control of the puck. Cornell won the faceoff and charged into the offensive zone, a scramble broke out in front of the net, and Trent Andison put a backhand shot past Shields. Only twenty-one seconds had elapsed.

"I remember coming into the dressing room afterwards," says Derraugh. "Everyone was so pumped up. As one of the leaders on the team, I was just trying to calm them down, because we had to win another one."

It was not to be—Michigan won the next two games to take the series. But the Big Red had proved they could take on one of the nation's top teams at their home rink and match their effort. "Our players had given everything," says McCutcheon. "It basically came down to Michigan having a little more depth and the home ice advantage." Cornell's final record was 18–11–3—but none of the players or their coach would ever forget that eighteenth win. And neither would the Michigan fans.

⁜ SIEVE! ⁜

In their 1991 NCAA playoff matchup, Michigan's players learned something about their feisty opponents from Ithaca—and their fans learned something from the Lynah Faithful who made the trek to Ann Arbor. "[The Cornell fans] were loud and they got their message across, and I think [our] fans kind of took it as a challenge," said Michigan alumnus Matt Thullen, quoted in a 2010 *Michigan Daily* article by Michael Florek. He continued: "We're the ones with the intimidating building. We're the home team. We're not going to let these guys come in and basically do anything [they want]."

That weekend, the Yost fans responded not only in volume but by learning some of the Faithful's cheers. "The number and variety of cheers that were taken vary, depending on the memory of each person that was there," reported Florek. "Some say that Steve Shields wasn't the only goalie who had his mother call to tell him he sucked. Others can only remember Cornell goaltender Jim Crozier getting hit with 'It's all your fault! It's all your fault!' added to the end of Michigan's already established goal count. But the most important lesson that Big Red crowd taught wasn't a specific chant—it was the attitude that a college hockey crowd should have."

Crozier clearly remembers hearing the Faithful at Yost. "Those games were during spring break, and I know that a lot of students changed their plans so they could attend," he says. "To see the number of Cornell fans

The traditions of the Lynah Faithful have been emulated by hockey fans at many other schools—including the University of Michigan. (Cornell Athletic Communications)

there was very special, and it really had an impact on the players—and on the Michigan fans."

Longtime Michigan coach Red Berenson has cited the influence of the Faithful numerous times over the years. "Red spoke about it at one of the coaches' conferences," says Doug Derraugh. "He was saying how they came away from that series with respect and admiration for the Cornell fans, and how their fans had tried to adopt a lot of those things. He said that really helped them to develop their fan support."

CORNELL 5, HARVARD 3
LYNAH RINK, ITHACA, NEW YORK, NOVEMBER 11, 1995

Stepping in as the new head coach for 1995–96 was Mike Schafer, who had been tri-captain of the 1986 ECAC champions and a defenseman with a take-no-prisoners attitude (which included once snapping a stick over his helmet during the introductions before a Harvard game). After graduating, he had been an assistant at Cornell before going to Western Michigan and serving under longtime head coach Bill Wilkinson for five years. On his return to Ithaca, Schafer immediately established three goals for his team: beat Harvard, pack Lynah Rink, and get home-ice advantage for the ECAC playoffs.

After the two victories over Harvard in the 1990 ECAC quarterfinals, defeating the Crimson had once again become a problem. In the twelve games against their rival since those postseason wins, the Big Red had a record of 0–9–3. So there was great anticipation in Ithaca when Harvard came to Lynah for the first home weekend. In a *Cornell Daily Sun* article on the day before the game, team captain Brad Chartrand '96 wrote: "The fish, the octopi, the noise—what a rush. . . . It's sure good to be home." He proved to be prophetic.

Looking back, Schafer says, "I figured that if we were going to have success, we needed to step up and win that game. It was important to our fans and our alumni and, of course, to our players. We had to show that we had the confidence to beat Harvard."

After the trout were tossed, the players introduced, and the national anthems played, Cornell took the lead at 3:58 of the first period when Matt Cooney '97 got a pass from Chartrand

---

(*facing page*) Senior captain Brad Chartrand, better known for his defense, scored a hat trick against Harvard. Although he went on to a successful career with the NHL's Los Angeles Kings, he says that game against the Crimson was "the top moment in my hockey career." (Cornell Athletic Communications)

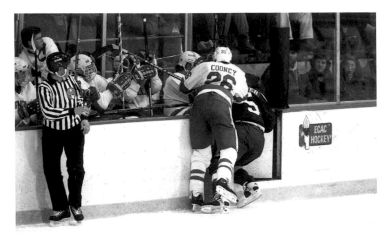

Forward Matt Cooney was not afraid of playing a physical game. He could also score—and he got the Big Red off to a good start, knocking in the game's first goal. Harvard evened the score soon after, but a shorthanded goal by P. C. Drouin put Cornell ahead for good. (Cornell Athletic Communications)

Early in the second period, Brad Chartrand (21) scored a shorthanded goal to put Cornell ahead 3–1. (© *Cornell Daily Sun*, used by permission)

and scored on Harvard goalie Tripp Tracy. "I was sneaking past their defenseman," says Cooney. "He had his stick tied up into me, but I managed to put the puck on net. I wasn't in a position to pick a corner, but I believe it went five hole."

A turnover after the ensuing faceoff allowed the Crimson to even the score only seventeen seconds later, but a shorthanded goal by P. C. Drouin '96 put the Big Red back in front. "We've changed our [penalty kill] system a little bit," said defenseman Steve Wilson '97 after the game. "We've been given the go-ahead to make some offensive opportunities, given the chance."

As if to prove that point, Chartrand put his team ahead 3–1 with another shorthanded goal at 1:44 of the second period. He was just getting started. He scored the next two goals, his third bringing a cascade of hats onto the ice. "I've played hockey since I was five years old and was lucky enough to play until I was thirty," says Chartrand. "Two moments stand out to me—and number one was scoring that hat trick against Harvard. The other was scoring the game-winning goal [for the Los Angeles Kings] against Patrick Roy in game 6 of the Stanley Cup play-offs. But I rank the Harvard hat trick above that, because I'm still good friends with the players on that team and it meant so much to the program. It really was the top moment in my hockey career."

The final score was 5–3. "As the last minutes ticked away, the Lynah crowd reached new heights of euphoria," wrote Adam Thompson in the *Daily Sun*. "When time ran out, the Red bench cleared and a few even climbed over the glass and onto the ice. The icers raised their sticks in salute of their supporters, who had played such a vital role in the win."

Many of the players on the 1995–96 team had been recruited by Brian McCutcheon, and at first they were not sure what to think of their new head coach (seated to the left of captain Brad Chartrand in the center of the first row). He won them over with his skill at learning how to best use their abilities to help the team win. (Cornell Athletic Communications)

Mike Schafer insisted that his players work out over the summer, and he implemented a tough training program as soon as they got to campus.
He wanted the team to get off to a strong start by beating Harvard in their early-season matchup at Lynah Rink. (Cornell Athletic Communications)

After the game, the head coach was pleased but circumspect. "We've taken a good step," Schafer said, "but we've got a lot of work ahead of us down the road." The new head coach had been determined to change the culture of Cornell hockey from the moment he arrived on campus. After three consecutive losing seasons, he wanted to give the program a fresh start and instill pride in his players. "When Mike came in, he put a lot of structure into the program," says Chartrand. "He sent us a workout program for the summer. It was mandatory to follow that and track your progress."

Once they got to campus, the players lifted weights at 6:30 a.m. three days a week. They were expected to go to class and maintain good academic records—or they wouldn't play. On the ice, Schafer carefully evaluated each player's abilities. "Brian McCutcheon had a system that he wanted to execute, and he applied the system to the players," says Mike Sancimino '96. "Schafe's approach was more like, 'Hey, you guys tell me what you are—are you a scorer, are you a defensive player?' He molded the system with that information. He was really good at identifying individual styles and building a system around them."

Schafer also emphasized the team's history. Soon after his players arrived for preseason practices, he had them take the championship trophies down from the shelves and polish them. Then he gave them some homework. "In the first week, we were all in the dressing room," says Kyle Knopp '99. "Mike came in and told us to research our number, and then come back and present to the rest of the team who was the best Cornell player ever to wear that number."

It paid off. When the regular season ended, the Big Red had

For the 1995–96 season, Mike Schafer returned to Cornell as the new head coach. After graduating, he had served as an assistant coach at Cornell and Western Michigan, and he was determined to bring a new attitude to the Big Red program. (Cornell Athletic Communications)

Freshman forward Kyle Knopp was impressed by Mike Schafer's emphasis on the history of the Cornell program. "I didn't know any of that stuff, like how many games Ken Dryden had won at Cornell," he says. "It was pretty cool to learn that history and get that pride about the school." (Cornell Athletic Communications)

a 17–8–4 record and was fourth in the conference. They had earned home ice for the quarterfinals of the ECAC playoffs—and they packed Lynah Rink for the games. The Big Red quickly disposed of Colgate in a best-of-three series, winning by scores of 8–3 and 8–1. They moved on to the semifinal game in Lake Placid, where they faced Clarkson; goaltender Jason Elliott '98 made twenty-seven saves, many of them spectacular, and Cornell prevailed 3–0.

In the ECAC championship game, Schafer's team faced . . . Harvard (of course). Although the Crimson had a losing record, they had upset ECAC regular-season champion Vermont to reach the final. And they were ready to reassert their supremacy over Cornell.

A record crowd of 8,300 was on hand in Olympic Arena when the rivals faced off. A misplay by Elliott gave Harvard a 1–0 lead only thirty-six seconds into the game—but apparently it served to focus the goaltender on his task. He would not surrender another goal. Cornell evened the score midway through the first on a goal by Cooney, and then took the lead at 2:06 of the second, when Sancimino grabbed his own rebound and scored what would prove to be the game winner.

Another apparent Cornell goal, on a shot from the point by Steve Wilson, was waved off for a crease violation, but it didn't matter. The Big Red played flawless defense the rest of the way, holding Harvard to three shots in the final period, and the buzzer sounded with the 2–1 score on the board. "It was a great outcome for the team and for the school," says Sancimino. "It was phenomenal."

Jason Elliott was named the tournament's MVP, following in the footsteps of fellow Cornell goalies Ken Dryden, Darren Eliot, and Doug Dadswell. In the four ECAC playoff games, he had made 104 saves on 109 shots. "Everything's come together for me," he said after receiving the honor. "[But] I think when an award like that is given to a goaltender, a lot of the credit has to be given to the team as a whole."

Although Cornell lost to Lake Superior State in the first round of the NCAA Tournament, there was a great deal of pride in Ithaca. Schafer had achieved his goals for the season, and the team was poised for greater success. "Our team has to recognize that it put Cornell back on the map, as far as being a nationally recognized program," said Schafer in the postgame press conference. "And that's where it belongs."

Cornell faced Harvard again in the ECAC final. A second-period goal by senior forward Mike Sancimino gave the Big Red a 2–1 lead—and that would be the final score, earning Mike Schafer his first ECAC championship as the head coach. (Cornell Athletic Communications)

Jason Elliott's outstanding performance in backstopping the Big Red to its eighth ECAC championship earned him tournament MVP honors. He was the fourth Cornell goaltender to be so honored, along with Ken Dryden, Darren Eliot, and Doug Dadswell. (Cornell Athletic Communications)

CORNELL 5, HARVARD 0
BRIGHT HOCKEY CENTER, CAMBRIDGE, MASSACHUSETTS, FEBRUARY 25, 1996

In 1992–93, Julie Andeberhan's first season as head coach, the Cornell women's team won two games. Three years later, they were on the verge of an Ivy League championship and their first trip to the ECAC playoffs. All that stood in the way was Harvard.

Andeberhan had been an outstanding player for the Crimson. In 1987–88, her senior year, Harvard won the Ivy League title and she was honored as Ivy League Player of the Year. But if she was feeling sentimental about her alma mater from her position behind the Cornell bench, it didn't show. Ever

---

(*facing page*) After the early success of the Cornell women's team, winners of six consecutive Ivy League championships under head coach Bill Duthie, the program had struggled. Between 1984 and 1993, the Big Red won only a single Ivy title and often finished with a losing record. (Cornell Athletic Communications)

the fierce competitor, she wanted to beat Harvard and win the championship.

The Cornell team was young but talented, with a strong contingent of eight freshmen and transfers. Leading the way for the first-year players were forwards Dana Antal '99 and Morag McPherson '99, who had both represented their provinces at the Canada Winter Games in the previous year. In goal, there was another pair of outstanding freshmen, Alanna Hayes '99 and Melissa Junkala '99. The preseason outlook in the Cornell Athletics media guide trumpeted that "there are high expectations that the resurgent program will take the next step in returning to the glory years of the past."

The head coach shared that view. "Julie pushed everybody to excel, not only physically but mentally," says Hayes, who became the team's primary goaltender and was the starter against Harvard. "For every game, she always had a strategy for getting

The 1995–96 women's team was known for its "never give up" attitude, as demonstrated here by Erin Schmalz's all-out effort to get the puck to a teammate. (© *Cornell Daily Sun*, used by permission)

Morag McPherson was one of four standout freshmen on the team, along with Dana Antal and goaltenders Alanna Hayes and Melissa Junkala. She would earn an assist on Antal's third-period goal by snagging a rebound of Antal's initial shot and sending a perfect pass back to her. (Cornell Athletic Communications)

us to work together and work hard, to understand that you have to keep digging and can never give up."

Going into the game, Cornell was tied with Brown for first place in the Ivy League standings. The championship went to the team with the best regular-season record against league opponents—there was no tournament—and one more win would clinch the title for the Big Red. They were 7–1–1 in Ivy contests and had posted shutouts of Yale and Northeastern in their last two games.

Against Harvard, Andeberhan wanted her team to come out fast. Forward Robin Thompson '97 obliged, taking a pass from linemate Antal and firing it past Harvard goaltender Jen Bowdoin at 8:10 of the first period. In the second, center Janna Dewar '97 added another goal. The crowd of two hundred or so, most of them Harvard supporters, sagged—but a few insistent voices could be heard, cheering on the Big Red. "No matter where you are," says Hayes, "if Cornell hockey is playing, there will be fans."

"The floodgates opened in the third period," reported Dan Babitz in the *Daily Sun*, "as Cornell scored three times to tighten its grasp on the Ivy League trophy." The first of those goals came from forward Erin Schmalz '98 at 2:14, and then Antal tallied just before the midway mark of the period. "When Erin scored the third goal, we all started to believe it was happening," said Andeberhan after the game, "but Dana's goal put it away."

The fourth goal came on an outstanding effort by the team's top scorer. The play began with a pass from McPherson that sent Antal across the blue line and into the offensive zone, where she fired a shot on net. "A nice save was made," wrote

Julie Andeberhan had been an outstanding player at Harvard, and she was hired by Cornell in 1993 as the new head coach. Although her team won only two games in her first year behind the bench, they were on the brink of another Ivy championship two years later. (Cornell Athletic Communications)

Alanna Hayes was outstanding in the championship game, making thirty-two saves to post her second shutout of the year. She is modest about her effort, saying, "It very much felt like a whole team win." (Cornell Athletic Communications)

Babitz, "but a hustling McPherson followed up on the play and slipped a pass to a turning Antal, who made good on her second try." Andeberhan praised the play, saying, "It was a perfect way to show the heart and the guts of this team."

Thompson would score again, at 14:59 of the third, with another assist from Antal, who would be named the Ivy League Rookie of the Year after a season in which she had seventeen goals and nineteen assists in twenty-two games. Hayes was flawless in goal, stopping thirty-two shots and recording her second shutout of the season. "I may have made a big save here and there," she says, "but I don't remember any glory moments for me. It very much felt like a whole team win. I loved playing the game and winning the championship. I loved representing Cornell."

In the post-game press conference, Andeberhan celebrated the dedication of her players. "All along, the Ivy title has been our goal," she said. "The girls came into the game believing that we can win, and showed that we wanted it."

There would be one more game. Cornell had finished fifth in the ECAC and qualified for the conference tournament, established in 1985, for the first time. Their opponent was Providence College. The Big Red fell to the Lady Friars 5–2 in a game played at Schneider Arena in Providence, but that did not diminish the luster of an outstanding season.

Forward Dana Antal, who was named Ivy League Rookie of the Year for 1995–96, passed to linemate Robin Thompson for the first goal in the championship game against Harvard. Later in the game, she would score a goal herself and get another assist. (Cornell Athletic Communications)

CORNELL 2, CLARKSON 1
OLYMPIC ARENA, LAKE PLACID, NEW YORK, MARCH 15, 1997

In 1996–97, graduation and injuries threatened to derail Mike Schafer's effort to win a second straight ECAC title. Nine seniors had moved on, including the captain, Brad Chartrand, who would play for the NHL's Los Angeles Kings for five years. Among the players remaining, a series of injuries had required constant lineup adjustments throughout the season—and team captain Matt Cooney went out with a concussion in the last regular-season game. After the ECAC quarterfinals against Harvard, he was joined on the sidelines by one of the team's top defensemen, Jeff Burgoyne '99, who had injured a knee.

And yet, there was Cornell in the ECAC final once again—shorthanded but determined. Their opponent, Clarkson, had finished in first place for the regular season, winning both games against Cornell. They had a potent offense led by Todd White, a Hobey Baker finalist who had scored thirty-eight goals that year, including a hat trick against Princeton in the semifinal. "I hope we saved our best game for [tonight]," said Schafer, "because we're going to need it."

Displaying what would become the trademark style for Schafer's teams, Cornell played a defense-first game against Clarkson, emphasizing close checking and airtight penalty killing. The Golden Knights had the man advantage six times and failed to score. Even better, the Big Red converted two of their six power plays, getting big goals from two defensemen. "Our special teams got going at the right time of the year," said Schafer after the game.

(facing page) Clarkson's Todd White, here facing off against Vinnie Auger, was an outstanding offensive player and Hobey Baker finalist. He had scored three goals against Princeton in the ECAC semifinal, but the Big Red defense kept him off the scoreboard. (Nancie Battaglia/Cornell Athletic Communications)

Jason Dailey got Cornell on the board first in the ECAC championship game, scoring a power-play goal late in the opening period. Darren Tymchyshyn (11) celebrated the moment. (© *Cornell Daily Sun,* used by permission)

Steve Wilson tallied the eventual game-winner in the second period, putting Cornell ahead 2–0. (© *Cornell Daily Sun,* used by permission)

Jason Dailey '98 scored the first Cornell goal, firing in a shot from a tough angle just as a power play was about expire late in the first period. Fellow blueliner Steve Wilson then netted the game winner midway through the second. "Wilson knocked a clearing attempt out of mid-air at the point, settled the puck and let fly from 40 feet," reported Tom Fleischman in the *Ithaca Journal.* "The puck sailed through a screen, caught the inside of the left post and fell into the goal for just his third of the season."

Looking back, Wilson says, "Most of the points I got were on assists, but I did chip in the odd goal. That was a big one." And it was all that goaltender Jason Elliott needed.

"As the game entered the third stanza, the icers fell into a defensive shell, weathering 12 Clarkson shots while registering only two of their own," wrote Adam Thompson in the *Daily Sun.* "Elliott especially stood out in the final period. His toughest save came with Steve Wilson in the box midway through the stanza. J. F. Houle crossed the puck to Matt Pagnutti, but the goalie stuck out his right pad to keep the defenseman from scoring into a nearly empty net."

The Golden Knights kept up the pressure, outshooting the Big Red thirty-two to twelve for the game, but they could manage only a single score, which came when Houle tallied with 6:42 left in the third. Even with their goalie pulled and the whole team crashing the net, they couldn't get another. The Big Red players kept checking them into the boards and clearing the puck. Icing was called repeatedly, stopping the clock and making the last few minutes seem to last forever for the Faithful, but the scoreboard read 2–1 when the final horn sounded.

"That was an incredible win because we had lost so many seniors," says Cooney. "After losing such a large number of great

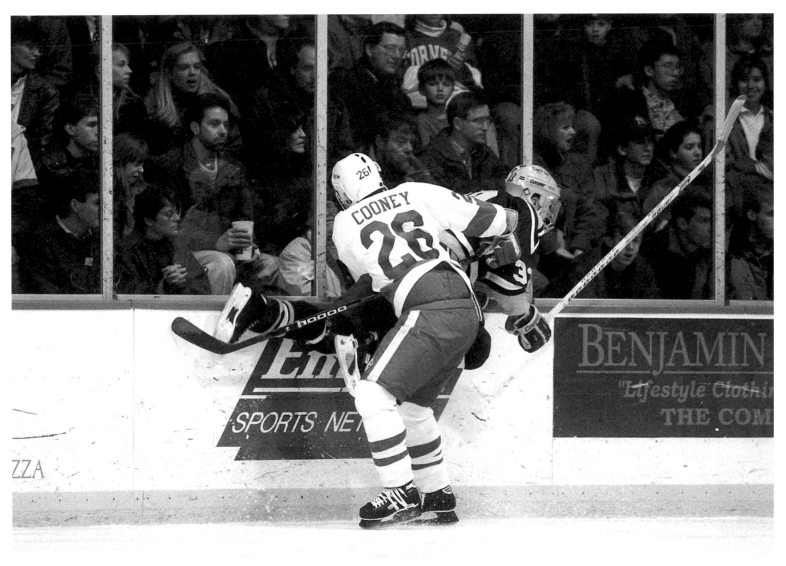

The 1996–97 Cornell team was plagued by injuries. Hard-hitting senior captain Matt Cooney, an important team leader, suffered a concussion in the last regular-season game and was unable to take the ice in the ECAC playoffs. (Cornell Athletic Communications)

Defenseman Steve Wilson (7) scored the game-winning goal in the second period of the ECAC championship game, firing a long shot that eluded Clarkson goalie Dan Murphy. Wilson had nineteen goals in his college career, but none was bigger. (Nancie Battaglia/Cornell Athletic Communications)

Jason Kendall (24) reaches for the puck between the skates of Vinnie Auger (19), who is battling with Clarkson's J. F. Houle. Houle scored the only goal for the Golden Knights, late in the third period. (Nancie Battaglia/Cornell Athletic Communications)

Three Jasons: in front of goalie Jason Elliott, Jason Kendall (24) and Jason Dailey (27) clear the puck. Elliott was named the tournament's MVP for the second year in a row, joining Ken Dryden as the only players to win back-to-back conference honors. (Nancie Battaglia/Cornell Athletic Communications)

players, I don't think that people expected us to have the horses again. The first [ECAC championship] took people by surprise, but the second one may have been just as surprising."

Schafer's defensive scheme had frustrated Todd White throughout the championship game and even aggravated him into committing a roughing penalty in the second period. "They were on him like glue," lamented Clarkson coach Mark Morris. "They played him tight, they played him smart. That's the type of hockey you've got to play to win in the playoffs."

Elliott was once again named the Most Valuable Player, joining distinguished company as one of only two players ever to win the award in two consecutive years. The other such honoree was Ken Dryden, in 1968 and 1969. "With the illustrious career that Ken Dryden had . . . it's such an honor," said Elliott after the game.

Once again, Cornell moved on to the NCAA Tournament—but this time, they got further. In the twelve-team, single-elimination format, the Big Red was the number 6 seed in the West Regional. In their first game, they faced Miami University at Van Andel Arena in Grand Rapids, Michigan. Although they had lost to the Redskins (as they were called then) at Lynah in late November, this time they prevailed, 4–2—with Cooney, cleared to play again, getting the final Cornell goal. Their season ended the next day, with a 6–2 loss to North Dakota, who would go on to win the national title.

The Big Red finished 21–9–5. In his first two years, Mike Schafer had led his team to a record of forty-two wins, eighteen losses, and nine ties—and two consecutive ECAC championships, making him the first Cornell coach to accomplish that feat since Ned Harkness.

Clarkson coach Mark Morris had led his team to two regular-season wins over Cornell on the way to earning the top seed in the tournament. But his high-scoring squad could not crack the Cornell defense in the final. (Courtesy of Clarkson Athletics)

"We're number one!" Mike Schafer's infant son John celebrates his father's big win. The smiling man at left is equipment manager Mike Teeter, who was inducted into the Cornell Athletics Hall of Fame in 2005 for his many years of volunteer service. (Nancie Battaglia/Cornell Athletic Communications)

Taking home the hardware (left to right): ECAC commissioner Joe Bertagna presented the Whitelaw Cup to Cornell's Jamie Papp, Matt Cooney, Steve Wilson, and Mike Schafer. It was Schafer's second ECAC title in a row and Cornell's ninth. (Nancie Battaglia/Cornell Athletic Communications)

CORNELL 3, HARVARD 2 OT
PEPSI ARENA, ALBANY, NEW YORK, MARCH 22, 2003

With thirty-eight seconds to go in the 2003 ECAC championship game, one of the greatest seasons in Cornell hockey history was in jeopardy. Despite winning the Ivy title, compiling the best ECAC regular-season record, and holding a number 2 national ranking, Cornell trailed Harvard 2–1. The Big Red net was empty, as Mike Schafer had pulled goalie David LeNeveu '05 for an extra attacker.

The year before, Cornell had gone into the ECAC championship game with the best record in the league—and had fallen, in double overtime, to Harvard. The game winner was scored by Tyler Kolarik, the same Crimson forward who had just deflected

---

(facing page) Junior forward Ryan Vesce was one of the stars of the 2002–03 Big Red team, scoring 45 points—but one of his biggest moments came on a faceoff in the ECAC championship game. (Courtesy of Adriano Manocchia)

a puck past LeNeveu, with only 3:46 left in the third period, to give his team the lead. The crowd in Albany's Pepsi Arena—overwhelmingly clad in Cornell colors—cheered frantically as the players lined up for a faceoff in the Harvard end: "Let's Go Red! Let's Go Red!"

After a battle for the puck, Harvard's Brett Nowak sent it down the ice, headed for the Cornell goal. The Faithful held their breath. As it crossed the red line, the puck went up on edge and rolled, veering to the right and missing the net. The Faithful exhaled. Icing was called, so the puck returned to the Harvard end for another faceoff.

Ryan Vesce '04 won the draw cleanly from Nowak—"I had his tendencies down," says Vesce, "and I was able to use that against him." He directed the puck to Mark McRae '03, who looked across the ice to fellow defenseman Doug Murray '03, in position to launch his powerful slap shot. But Harvard's Dominic

With the ECAC championship on the line, Cornell trailed Harvard 2–1 with less than a minute remaining. Ryan Vesce won a crucial faceoff and was able to send the puck to Mark McRae. (Cornell Athletic Communications)

Moore had anticipated the play; he moved toward Murray, ready to intercept. McRae reacted quickly, skating into the slot behind a screen of Cornell players. He saw an opening—and fired a hard, low shot. The Faithful erupted as the red light went on.

"I took a couple of steps to the middle, and it just opened up on the far side," says McRae. "The goalie couldn't see [around the screening players]. Taking an extra step opened up that side of the net. I had my head up and saw it the whole way—just fired it in."

There were still thirty-three seconds remaining. Harvard won the faceoff at center ice and moved quickly into the offensive zone. LeNeveu had to make one more big save to force overtime—and, of course, he did. The buzzer sounded to end regulation.

The extra time was short. Harvard came out on the attack, firing three quick shots. LeNeveu directed the last one to the corner, where Mark McRae battled a Harvard player and fell on the puck. The referee blew his whistle for a faceoff. Cornell gained control, and the puck came across the ice to McRae. He passed to winger Sam Paolini '03, who had started up the left side. Paolini raced up ice along the boards—"He was flying," says McRae—slipped past Harvard defenseman Kenny Smith, and fired a shot. It sailed over the outstretched glove of Crimson goalie Dov Grumet-Morris and into the net at 1:23 of overtime.

"And as soon as I had the puck, the defenseman was in my face," says Paolini. "I had to make a move and walk around him. Grumet-Morris was a small goalie, and my shot went high glove. He gave me a lot of room there."

The next day, in a special Sunday edition of the *Ithaca Journal*,

Mark McRae received the puck from Ryan Vesce and quickly evaluated the situation. Seeing that Harvard's Dominic Moore had anticipated a pass to Doug Murray, he skated into the slot and took a screened shot that beat goalie Dov Grumet-Morris to tie the game. (Courtesy of Adriano Manocchia)

In the overtime, Sam Paolini received a cross-ice pass from Mark McRae. He streaked up the left side, eluded a Harvard defenseman, and fired the game-winning shot over the shoulder of Grumet-Morris. (© *Cornell Daily Sun*, used by permission)

Sam Paolini was mobbed by his teammates after his game-winner. Cornell had completed a seemingly impossible comeback, winning in overtime after trailing with only thirty-eight seconds to go. (Courtesy of Adriano Manocchia)

Goalie David LeNeveu was named the MVP of the ECAC Tournament. It was one of many honors for his outstanding season; he also received the Ken Dryden Award as best ECAC goalie and was named ECAC co-player of the year and first-team All-American. (Courtesy of Adriano Manocchia)

After the game, Mike Schafer and assistant coach Brent Brekke raised the Whitelaw Cup and saluted their players, who had won Cornell's tenth ECAC championship and advanced to the NCAA Tournament. (Courtesy of Adriano Manocchia)

Christopher Feaver reported: "As soon as the puck rippled in the top right corner of the net, Paolini hung a left, then went into a euphoric knee-slide as the rest of the Cornell team mobbed him near the boards at center ice and much of the pro-Cornell crowd of 8,296 erupted in celebration."

The Big Red's dramatic victory, combined with a loss by then top-ranked Colorado College in the WCHA tournament, vaulted Cornell to number 1 in the national polls for the first time ever—and made them the top seed in the NCAA Tournament. When the pairings were announced, there was some grumbling in Ithaca, as Cornell had to face Minnesota State–Mankato, a number 14 seed rather than a number 15 or 16, which would have been expected as the opponent for the number 1 seed.

It didn't matter. In the first game of the NCAA East Regional at the Dunkin' Donuts Center in Providence, Rhode Island, the Big Red trounced Mankato 5–2. Mike Knoepfli '05 had two goals and an assist, Shane Hynes '06 had two goals, and Paolini scored again. Vesce got an assist on Paolini's goal for his one-hundredth career point, making him the first Cornell player to reach that milestone as a junior since Joe Nieuwendyk.

Up next was Boston College. The Eagles had finished the regular season tied with the University of New Hampshire at the top of the Hockey East standings and defeated Ohio State 1–0 in the first game of the tournament. Not surprisingly the game was a nail-biter that went, once again, to overtime, tied 1–1.

Both squads had good chances in the first OT, but the goalies were up to the challenge, stopping every shot. By then, the pace of the game and the warm temperature of the building were beginning to take a toll. "A lot of guys had bad cramps,"

Matt McRae's hard-angle shot in the second overtime defeated Boston College in the final of the NCAA East Regional and sent the Big Red to the Frozen Four. (Courtesy of Adriano Manocchia)

Co-captain Doug Murray was honored as the ECAC's Defensive Defenseman of the Year. One of the most hard-nosed blueliners ever to play for Cornell, he was drafted by the NHL's San Jose Sharks and had an eleven-year professional career. (Courtesy of Adriano Manocchia)

In the NCAA semifinal at Buffalo's HSBC Arena, the Big Red trailed UNH 3–2 and mounted an all-out attack after goalie LeNeveu was pulled. A shot by Stephen Bâby appeared to be headed for the corner of the net, but it bounced off goalie Mike Ayers's mask and went over the crossbar. (Courtesy of Adriano Manocchia)

On April 17, 2003, a celebration of the season was held at Lynah Rink. Mike Schafer and co-captains Murray and Bâby raised three new banners to the rafters. (Courtesy of Adriano Manocchia)

Rink announcer Arthur Mintz served as emcee of the campus celebration. (Courtesy of Adriano Manocchia)

says Paolini. "Guys were getting IVs between the overtime periods. We were really tired."

When the players returned for the second OT, Cornell controlled the early action. With just over one minute elapsed, forward Matt McRae '03—Mark's twin brother—carried the puck across the blue line and down the right side. "I was going full tilt, and the defensemen were trying to read the gap on me," says McRae. "I think they slightly misread it—and their legs, I'm sure, were getting quite heavy. There was that extra bit of time to get space coming around, where I had a shot."

Seeing a small opening on the near side, McRae lifted a shot over goalie Matti Kaltiainen's shoulder to win the game. "We played a lot of three-on-three with the coaches [in practice]," says McRae. "There had been a similar kind of tough-angle shot that had gone in early in the year, in one of those three-on-three games. I guess that's why I thought of that shot."

Cornell advanced to the Frozen Four at HSBC Arena in Buffalo, New York, where they met UNH in the semifinal. The Big Red appeared to take the early lead on a goal by Shane Palahicky '03, only to have it disallowed. After a lengthy video review, the officials ruled that it was struck with a high stick. (This remains a subject of controversy.) The Wildcats then jumped ahead 3–0. Cornell battled back, scoring two goals and dominating play until the final seconds, when a hard shot by co-captain Stephen Bâby '03 deflected off goalie Mike Ayers's mask and prevented the Big Red from forcing another overtime.

It was a disappointing end to what many had hoped would be a national championship season, but it did not diminish what the Big Red accomplished that year. Along with the banners that were added to the Lynah rafters, the team brought home a truckload of individual awards. Mike Schafer was named ECAC Coach of the Year for the second time in a row, and ECAC honors also went to Doug Murray, Defensive Defenseman of the Year; Stephen Bâby, Defensive Forward of the Year; David LeNeveu, Ken Dryden Award (best goalie), Co-Player of the Year, and Tournament MVP.

If there were any doubts remaining about Mike Schafer's ability to elevate his team to national prominence, the 2002–03 Big Red erased them. They ended the season with a 30–5–1 record, the most-ever wins by a Cornell hockey team to that point. They had a perfect 15–0 record at Lynah and were the top defensive unit in the nation. "When our players look back, they can't doubt their work ethic or their performance," said Schafer after the season-ending game. "We had our opportunities, we went for it, and that's the definition of success."

The Cleary Cup (left) and the Whitelaw Cup were on display at the celebration, honoring Cornell as the 2002–03 champions of both the ECAC regular season and tournament. (Courtesy of Adriano Manocchia)

Goal! Thanks to a screen from Shane Hynes (28) and Byron Bitz (29), a slap shot from Charlie Cook beat Harvard goalie Dov Grumet-Morris in the second period of the 2005 ECAC championship game. (Courtesy of Ned Dykes, Cornell Hockey Association)

CORNELL 3, HARVARD 1
PEPSI ARENA, ALBANY, NEW YORK, MARCH 19, 2005

In the 2005 ECAC Tournament, Harvard defeated Colgate 4–3 in a grueling double-overtime game to reach the final against Cornell. Surely, the Crimson players would be fatigued as they took the ice on Saturday night—and the Cornell players, winners of a relatively easy 3–0 semifinal against Vermont, would have the edge.

Defying that conventional wisdom, Harvard jumped ahead, scoring the game's first goal at 18:23 of the first period. "Dylan Reese let loose a shot from near the blue line during a power play," wrote Christopher Feaver in the *Ithaca Journal*, "that appeared to deflect off a Cornell player and sneak past Cornell goalie David McKee '07. The goal snapped a streak of 28 consecutive power plays the Big Red had killed off."

If that goal unsettled the Cornell players, they quickly regained their composure. In the second period, they outshot Harvard 14–2, scoring twice. The first goal came when forward Daniel Pegoraro '06 broke into the Harvard zone and pulled a defender out of position with a fake, then centered the puck to Paul Varteressian '05. His quick shot eluded Harvard goalie Dov Grumet-Morris and tied the game at the 9:35 mark. A hooking penalty then put Cornell on the power play, and a pass from Matt Moulson '06 led to a blue-line blast from defenseman Charlie Cook '05 that eluded a screened Grumet-Morris and found the net.

"Moulson was a pure goal scorer," says Cook. "He had the ability to come one step over the blue line and pick a corner on a goalie. Teams knew that—so when we were running our power play, they respected Matt. And any time they sat on him, the puck would come back to me [at the point]."

In the third, Harvard managed to kill a five-on-three, but the Big Red controlled the puck for much of the period—and Cook struck for another man-advantage goal, once again one-timing

For the 2005 ECAC Tournament, the Lynah Faithful and the pep band traveled to Albany's Pepsi Arena. After blanking Vermont 3–0 in the semifinal, Cornell once again faced Harvard for the championship. (Courtesy of Ned Dykes, Cornell Hockey Association)

Sophomore David McKee continued the Cornell tradition of outstanding goaltending with a championship on the line. In the 2005 ECAC playoffs, he allowed only three goals in four games. (Courtesy of Ned Dykes, Cornell Hockey Association)

Senior forward Paul Varteressian scored the first Cornell goal in the final, tying the game at 1–1 in the second period. (© *Cornell Daily Sun*, used by permission)

Defenseman Charlie Cook scored the game-winner for Cornell, taking a pass from Matt Moulson on the power play and blasting a shot from the point. (© *Cornell Daily Sun*, used by permission)

During a timeout, head coach Mike Schafer outlined his strategy for defending against Harvard's extra-attacker offense at the end of the game. (Courtesy of Ned Dykes, Cornell Hockey Association)

Cook's hard shot goes past Crimson goalie Dov Grumet-Morris, and Shane Hynes (28) celebrates. (© *Cornell Daily Sun*, used by permission)

a pass from Moulson to make the score 3–1. "We had a really good power play that year," says Moulson. "Charlie had a big shot, and in that game, he had two bombs that were the big goals for us."

Still, it was a close game—and the Big Red's longtime rivals gave it all they had in the final period. "With about seven minutes remaining in the game and Harvard on a power play, the Crimson peppered McKee with several shots from just outside the crease," wrote Owen Bochner '05 in the *Daily Sun*. "At one point, McKee appeared to be drawn away from the net, allowing Harvard's Dan Murphy an open shot on goal. However, the Cornell netminder was able to cover the puck with his body."

Harvard coach Ted Donato pulled Grumet-Morris with just

Charlie Cook (7) scored his second power-play goal in the third period.
(Courtesy of Ned Dykes, Cornell Hockey Association)

over four minutes remaining, but to no avail. The extra-attacker offense could not get the puck past McKee, who was unfazed by the Crimson's final assault. "The guys played great in front of me in that one," he says. "I think Harvard had only two or three good scoring chances."

After the game, Donato admitted that his team's lengthy battle in the semifinal had affected his players. "Friday's double-overtime game was a factor," he said. "How could it not be a factor? I prefer not to rely on excuses. They outplayed us tonight."

The Pepsi Arena crowd of 8,637 was once again overwhelmingly in favor of Cornell, and the Faithful celebrated the victory with a deafening salute of the Big Red players as they circled the ice with the Whitelaw Cup. Total attendance for the weekend had exceeded 16,000—the most for an ECAC championship since 1992, the last year that the tournament had been held in Boston Garden.

It was Cornell's eleventh ECAC title. "I remember going into Lynah on the very first day [as a freshman], and there was a spot in the locker room that had photographs of all the ECAC champions up on the wall," says Cook. "I said to myself, *Oh man, it would be amazing to have '05 up there.* And I know my classmates felt the same way. So from day one, everything we did, whether it was on the ice or off, was around winning. Whatever it took, whatever was asked."

Cook was named the Most Outstanding Player, and he was joined on the all-tournament team by McKee, Moulson, and Pegoraro. In the four ECAC playoff games, McKee had two shutouts, a 0.71 goals-against average, and a .970 save percentage.

After time expired, the Big Red players celebrated their victory behind the Cornell goal. (Courtesy of Ned Dykes, Cornell Hockey Association)

As the Lynah Faithful cheered, David McKee consoled his Harvard counterpart, Dov Grumet-Morris, who was on the losing end to Cornell in both 2003 and 2005. (His team did win the 2004 ECAC championship.) (Courtesy of Ned Dykes, Cornell Hockey Association)

Charlie Cook was named the Most Outstanding Player of the 2005 ECAC Tournament. (© *Cornell Daily Sun*, used by permission)

He was named a Hobey Baker finalist and first-team All-American after an outstanding season in which he had ten shutouts—breaking David LeNeveu's record.

The ECAC championship game was the twentieth straight in which Schafer's team had not given up more than two goals. That streak was extended in the NCAA Tournament, where Cornell defeated Ohio State 3–2 in the West Regional at Mariucci Arena in Minneapolis, getting a game-winning goal from Mike Iggulden '05 after falling behind 2–0. The next day, in the battle for a trip to the Frozen Four, they dropped an overtime heartbreaker, 2–1, to a strong Minnesota team playing on its home ice, to finish the season at 27–5–3.

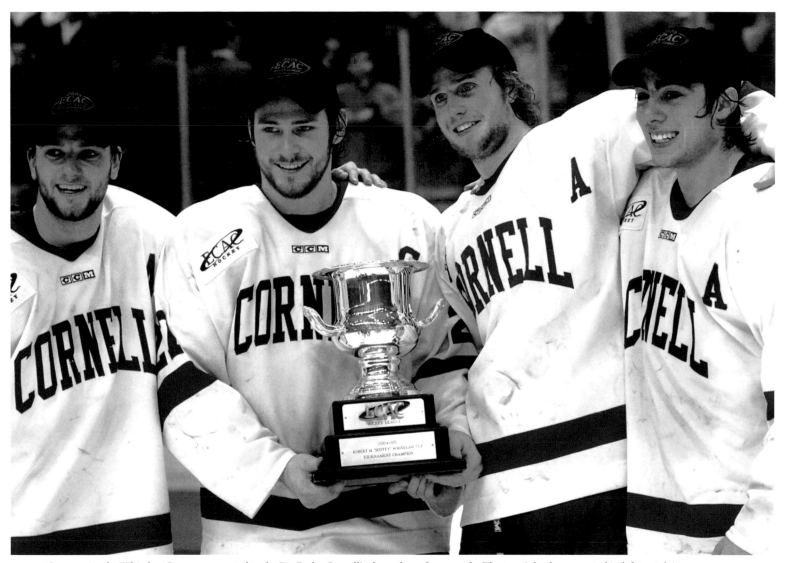

Once again, the Whitelaw Cup was presented to the Big Red—Cornell's eleventh conference title. The team's leaders accepted it (left to right): assistant captain Charlie Cook, captain Mike Knoepfli, and assistant captains Mike Iggulden and Matt Moulson. (© *Cornell Daily Sun*, used by permission)

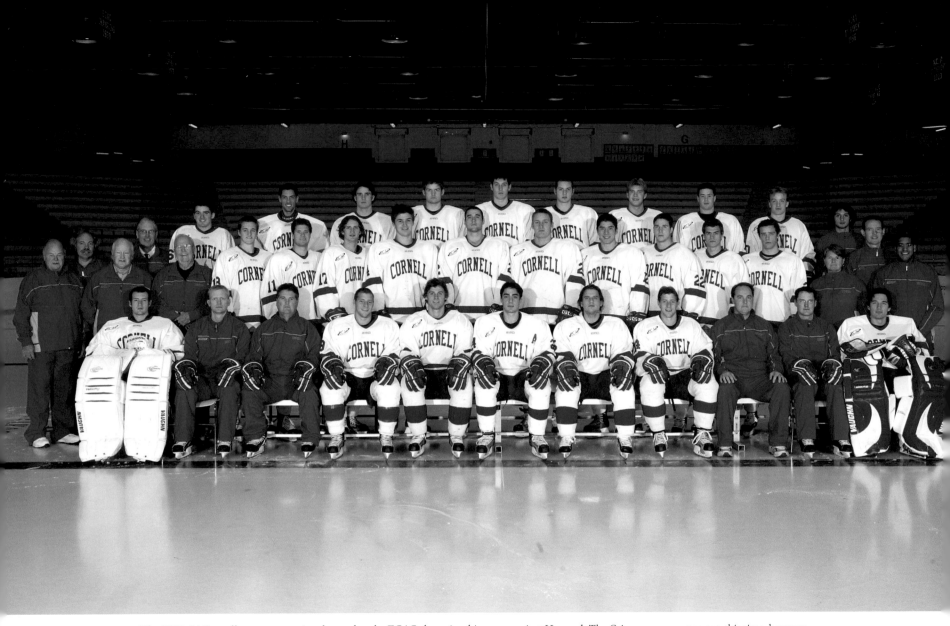

The 2005–06 Cornell team once again advanced to the ECAC championship game against Harvard. The Crimson came out on top this time, however—but the Big Red were selected for the NCAA Tournament, where they defeated Colorado College and faced Wisconsin in the Midwest Regional final. (Cornell Athletic Communications)

WISCONSIN 1, CORNELL 0 3OT
RESCH CENTER, GREEN BAY, WISCONSIN, MARCH 26, 2006

In Mike Schafer's final year as a player, Cornell went to overtime in a dozen games, including a 3–2 thriller over Clarkson to win the ECAC Tournament. Twenty years later, his 2005–06 squad looked as if it might be trying to surpass that total, enduring six OT games in the regular season and then winning a pair of double-overtime playoff heart-stoppers against Clarkson at Lynah to advance to the ECAC championship round in Albany. They polished off Colgate 2–0 in the semifinal—no extra time needed—and moved on to face Harvard, once again, in the final. Unfortunately, they ran into a red-hot team that scored three power-play goals in the first period and never looked back, defeating the Big Red 6–2 to win the ECAC title.

Even so, Cornell was one of the sixteen teams selected to go to the NCAA Tournament. They defeated Colorado College 3–2 in the first round of the Midwest Regional, coming back from a 2–0 deficit to advance to the regional final—and one of

the epic battles in NCAA hockey history. Their opponent was Wisconsin, the tournament's number 1 seed, playing in their home state in front of thousands of passionate Badger fans.

For three periods, the two teams clad in red and white battled back and forth. There were good scoring opportunities for each, but the goaltenders, Cornell's David McKee and Wisconsin's Brian Elliott, were—to use an old hockey saying—standing on their heads. They made save after save, many of them spectacular.

Wisconsin came close to ending it in the third. "With 3:02 remaining, the Badgers could have swiped the game on its fifth power play of the night after sophomore Topher Scott was penalized for holding," wrote Brian Tsao '06 in the *Daily Sun*. "However, McKee blocked shots from Andrew Joudrey, Tom Gilbert and Jeff Likens and made the stop of the night when he made an acrobatic kick save to knock away a close-range

The Big Red were led by senior captain Matt Moulson, who scored 148 points in his college career and was drafted by the NHL's Pittsburgh Penguins. (Courtesy of Ned Dykes, Cornell Hockey Association)

Robbie Earl one-timer."

After sixty minutes of play, the score remained 0–0. The Cornell players, perhaps thinking back to those two double-overtime ECAC playoff wins against Clarkson, remained confident. "We all thought we were going to win that game," says McKee.

After one overtime period, the game remained scoreless. After a second, that was still true. A third overtime period began. Both teams came close to ending it, with shots that caromed off the post. "Both of us had our chances," says Schafer. "We got tired at one point and Wisconsin really took it to us, and then it seemed like they hit a wall and we started taking it to them. It went back and forth."

Midway through the third OT, Cornell's Tyler Mugford '09 and Wisconsin's Davis Drewiske were given matching penalties for roughing. In the resulting four-on-four, Wisconsin dumped the puck into the Cornell end. McKee went behind the net to retrieve it. He fired it around the boards, thinking that a teammate would pick it up and carry it out of the zone.

But Wisconsin's Josh Engel won the race to the puck, and he sent a quick pass into the high slot, right to the stick of teammate Jack Skille. His one-timer went over McKee's left shoulder, sending Wisconsin's fans into exhausted elation. "While the Badgers were basking in glory," reported the *Ithaca Journal*, "the Big Red was left standing in stunned silence."

The official playing time was 111 minutes and 13 seconds—with intermissions, nearly five hours on the clock. McKee had made fifty-nine saves and Elliott, who was named the Regional Tournament MVP, had made forty. Ninety-nine saves on a hundred shots. "Both goalies were extraordinary," says Moulson,

Against Wisconsin, David McKee had one of the greatest games ever played by a college goaltender. In a tense contest that stretched into a third overtime period, he made fifty-nine saves—some of them on point-blank shots. (Courtesy of Ned Dykes, Cornell Hockey Association)

At the other end of the ice, Wisconsin goalie Brian Elliott was also outstanding, stopping forty Cornell shots. (Courtesy of Ned Dykes, Cornell Hockey Association)

As the teams prepared for overtime, Mike Schafer discussed strategy with his players. Junior forward Mark McCutcheon (10)—son of former Cornell player and coach Brian McCutcheon—listened intently. (Courtesy of Ned Dykes, Cornell Hockey Association)

The intensity of the action can be seen on the faces of Wisconsin's Robbie Earl (10) and Cornell's Mitch Carefoot (11) as they wait for a faceoff. (Courtesy of Ned Dykes, Cornell Hockey Association)

The referee signals that the puck is in the net. Wisconsin wins on the only goal of the game, scored by Jack Skille after 111 minutes and 13 seconds of heart-stopping action. "It was a tough way for me to end my college career," says Matt Moulson. (© Neil Ament, used by permission)

The scoreboard sums it up: one hundred shots, one goal. (Courtesy of Ned Dykes, Cornell Hockey Association)

the team's senior captain. "We hit some posts, and [Wisconsin] had some chances. It was a tough way for me to end my college career."

Although McKee was a junior, it turned out to be his final game for Cornell as well. Two weeks later, he signed a professional contract with the NHL's Mighty Ducks of Anaheim. "I still haven't found the words to describe how that game felt," he says. "The hardest part was the mental aspect, especially when you're getting that deep in overtime. Make a save and wait, and try to make the next save. Brian Elliott was making some amazing saves at the other end. I thought Matt Moulson was going to score, late in the third period, but Brian stuck his left leg out and made a ridiculous save. Took my breath away. It was definitely bittersweet, because we lost, but it was also the most enjoyable game I ever played."

In the postgame press conference, Wisconsin coach Mike Eaves said, "That was a head-to-head goalie exhibition that may never be matched again." His team went on to win the NCAA championship, defeating Maine and then Boston College to secure the title—but neither game came close to the intensity, or the length, of the unforgettable one they had played against Cornell.

The exhausted players lined up to shake hands after the game. Wisconsin would go on to win the national championship, while the Cornell players would have only their enduring memories of an unforgettable battle. (Courtesy of Ned Dykes, Cornell Hockey Association)

As the Big Red players gave their final salute to the Lynah Faithful, appreciative Wisconsin fans joined in the applause. (Courtesy of Ned Dykes, Cornell Hockey Association)

BOSTON UNIVERSITY 6, CORNELL 3
MADISON SQUARE GARDEN, NEW YORK CITY, NOVEMBER 24, 2007

The idea for reviving the Boston University rivalry with a show-case game at Madison Square Garden originated at BU—but it was enthusiastically supported by Cornell. Robert Brown, who had been named BU's president in 2005, wanted to have an event in New York City where he could connect with the school's alumni. A hockey game seemed to be a natural, so Mike Lynch, BU's athletic director, talked it over with hockey coach Jack Parker. He liked the idea, but was concerned about the size of "The World's Most Famous Arena," which has a capacity of 18,200 for hockey.

"I said, 'Let me think about it,'" says Parker. "And then I thought, *You know who we could play where we might draw 10,000? Cornell.* So I had Mike Lynch call [Andy Noel], the AD

at Cornell, and I called Mike Schafer and said, 'How about playing a renewal of the rivalry at Madison Square Garden?'"

Schafer loved the idea of giving his team the experience of playing in a large urban arena in front of thousands of Cornell fans: "From a coaching standpoint, you don't have to worry about motivating. You don't have to worry about getting guys fired up to play."

With the athletic directors and coaches from both schools solidly behind the idea, the wheels began to turn. It took two years to get everything in place for Red Hot Hockey, as the game was billed, but there was great anticipation in both the Cornell and BU communities as the game day approached. "BU vs. Cornell anywhere would be a big story, but BU vs. Cornell at Madison Square Garden is huge," said Parker before the game. "The players on both teams will get to experience that type of atmosphere against a big rival in a game they should remember for a long, long time."

(facing page) In November 2007, Cornell faced off against Boston University at Madison Square Garden in a revival of their intense rivalry from the 1960s and '70s. (Courtesy of Ned Dykes, Cornell Hockey Association)

Before the first Red Hot Hockey game at Madison Square Garden, legendary Cornell coach Ned Harkness (right) was escorted to center ice by John Hughes, one of the captains of the undefeated 1970 team. (Courtesy of Ned Dykes, Cornell Hockey Association)

On November 24, 2007, "The World's Most Famous Arena" was packed with hockey fans—almost all of them wearing red, but about two-thirds of them rooting for Cornell. (Courtesy of Ned Dykes, Cornell Hockey Association)

The ceremonial puck drop was performed by Ned Harkness and his rival from the '60s, former Boston University coach Jack Kelley. (Courtesy of Ned Dykes, Cornell Hockey Association)

With the teams lined up and an honor guard at attention, a trumpeter stepped out to perform "The Star-Spangled Banner." (Courtesy of Ned Dykes, Cornell Hockey Association)

BU got off to a quick start, scoring three first-period goals. Goalie Ben Scrivens played them much tougher after that, making thirty-six saves in the game, but the big early lead was too much for Cornell to overcome. (Courtesy of Ned Dykes, Cornell Hockey Association)

The concerns about getting a good crowd proved to be unfounded: the game was a sellout. The building was buzzing with excitement as Ned Harkness and former BU coach Jack Kelley walked out on a red carpet for the ceremonial puck drop. Harkness was escorted by John Hughes, one of the captains of Cornell's undefeated 1970 team. The players were introduced, videos flashed on the big screen, and a trumpeter played the national anthem. The huge crowd—which appeared to be about two-to-one in favor of Cornell fans—roared as the game began.

"For one night, the Lynah Faithful—those dedicated souls who experience the throes of an entire Cornell men's hockey season as if they were on the team itself—annexed the Big Apple," wrote Brandon Thomas in the *Ithaca Journal*. "And it was clear from the moment sophomore goalie Ben Scrivens '10 led the Big Red onto the ice for warm-ups just which team the majority of the crowd was pulling for. It was one heck of a Garden party."

Until the game started, anyway. BU's offense came out in high gear, beating the Cornell players to the puck and firing shot after shot at Scrivens. Three of them ended up in the net, and the Terriers had a commanding lead midway through the opening period. "I think BU had a little bit of an upper hand on us," says Topher Scott. "They play the Beanpot every year, so they had more experience [playing in a large arena]." (The Beanpot is an

Co-captain Topher Scott, who would later become an assistant coach for the Big Red, says his team may have been distracted by the atmosphere in the big arena at the beginning of the game. "We were looking up into the crowd, soaking in the moment," he says, "and forgot to compete for a few minutes." (Courtesy of Ned Dykes, Cornell Hockey Association)

annual tournament played in February in Boston's TD Garden by BU, Boston College, Harvard, and Northeastern.) "We were looking up into the crowd, soaking in the moment, and forgot to compete for a few minutes."

The Cornell players regained their focus in the second period, scoring a power-play goal on a deflection by talented freshman Riley Nash '11. But just as momentum appeared to be swinging, a tripping penalty gave BU a man-advantage opportunity. They cashed it in to push their lead to 4–1.

Any questions about the final outcome were answered at 1:17 of the third, when BU's Colin Wilson tallied to make it 5–1. Cornell got goals from Scott and Jared Seminoff '09 to inch closer, but an empty-net goal by BU's Bryan Ewing with 23.7 seconds remaining made it 6–3. The final score was a bit deceptive, as Scrivens had played an outstanding game, making thirty-six saves, and puck possession was fairly even after BU's opening outburst.

Although the Cornell players were disappointed about losing the game, it was an indelible experience. "That's every kid's dream," says Scott, "to go out and play in front of almost 20,000 people. And to have a college atmosphere in a rink that big, hearing the crowd chanting 'Let's Go Red!' It was unbelievable."

After the game, *Daily Sun* sportswriter Yael Borofsky '08 saluted the large Cornell contingent in the crowd, writing: "No offense to the Lynah Faithful, but prior to this weekend, I was certain that outside of this loud but relatively small demographic, there aren't many people on this campus who would call themselves diehard Red fans. On Saturday, it was clear by the number of students and alumni singing the alma mater with gusto that we have a little more school pride than we receive credit for. Only

Freshman forward Riley Nash, seen here battling for the puck behind the BU net, got Cornell on the scoreboard with a second-period goal on the power play. (Patrick Shanahan/Cornell Athletic Communications)

The Cornell fans behind the BU net were enthusiastic about Riley Nash's goal. Goalie Brett Bennett looked up, as if to say, "Where did that come from?" (Courtesy of Ned Dykes, Cornell Hockey Association)

Third-period tallies by Topher Scott and Jared Seminoff pulled Cornell closer, but a BU empty-net goal in the last minute made the final score 6–3 in favor of the Terriers. (Courtesy of Ncd Dykes, Cornell Hockey Association)

people who really care about Red hockey would make up the majority of a sold-out 18,200-seat arena that doesn't even sell out when the Rangers play there."

In addition to showing the high level of support for Cornell's team, the game proved to be an important milestone for college hockey. What was initially seen as a one-off showcase has become a regular series, with Cornell meeting BU at Madison Square Garden on Thanksgiving weekend every other year, and many other intercollegiate games have been played at the famed venue since the first Red Hot Hockey contest. By showing what could be done at a major big-city arena, the two old rivals opened the door to a new era of visibility and popularity for college hockey.

Although there had been some concern about how well a college hockey game would draw in a large urban arena like Madison Square Garden, the scoreboard tells the story: attendance was 18,200—a sellout. (Courtesy of Ned Dykes, Cornell Hockey Association)

Cornell's Colin Greening (15) came close to scoring on this play, but his shot was turned away by BU goalie Brett Bennett. (Courtesy of Ned Dykes, Cornell Hockey Association)

The Big Red players were disappointed by the final score, but it was an unforgettable experience for them. "That's every kid's dream," says Topher Scott, "to go out and play in front of almost twenty thousand people." (Courtesy of Ned Dykes, Cornell Hockey Association)

CORNELL 4, CLARKSON 3 OT (WOMEN)
LYNAH RINK, ITHACA, NEW YORK, MARCH 7, 2010

CORNELL 3, UNION 0 (MEN)
TIMES UNION CENTER, ALBANY, NEW YORK, MARCH 20, 2010

This was a banner year for Cornell athletics. The men's basketball team won its third straight Ivy League championship and advanced to the Sweet Sixteen in the NCAA Tournament. The wrestling team finished second in the country, and Kyle Dake '13 won the national title at 141 pounds. And for the first time in program history, both the women's and men's hockey teams won an ECAC championship in the same season.

For the women, it was a surprising achievement after a long string of losing seasons. "We weren't even expected to make the playoffs," says head coach Doug Derraugh. "But that team worked hard, worked for each other, competed hard in practice,

---

(facing page) The 2009–10 season was outstanding for both the men's team and the women's team, which featured sophomore forward Kendice Ogilvie (4), the hero of the ECAC championship game against Clarkson. (Cornell Athletic Communications)

and wanted to get better each and every day." Their season started inauspiciously, with a pair of 4–1 losses at Lynah Rink to Mercyhurst. But Derraugh could see beyond the scores. "I remember coming into the locker room with the other coaches after the second game and saying to them that we were going to be really good this year," he recalls. "It was just a feeling I had after the way we played that first weekend."

He was right. The Big Red women vanquished one opponent after another, taking their last seven games in a row to secure the regular-season ECAC title. They then dispatched RPI to advance to the conference championship game against Clarkson, held at Lynah.

It looked as if this would be an easy win when Cornell jumped out to a 3–0 lead on goals by Catherine White '12, Laura Fortino '13, and Chelsea Karpenko '12. But then Clarkson started to chip away, getting a goal from Danielle Boudreau

Goaltender Amanda Mazzotta led her teammates onto the ice for the 2010 ECAC championship game against Clarkson at Lynah Rink. She would make thirty-one saves. (Courtesy of Ned Dykes, Cornell Hockey Association)

near the end of the second period. A power-play goal early in the third made it 3–2, and then Boudreau struck again, with 3:54 remaining, to tie the game.

"I guess I decided to take a nap going into the third," says goalie Amanda Mazzotta '12 with a chuckle. "But that was the cool part about our group—I don't think we were rattled one bit by going into overtime. We were just prepared to go out and get the next one."

In the OT, the Big Red women took only one shot on goal. That was all they needed. On the forecheck, co-captain Liz Zorn '10 captured the puck behind the Clarkson net and fed it to linemate Kendice Ogilvie '12, whose shot went over the shoulder of Clarkson goalie Lauren Dahm to end the game at 7:52. The Faithful crowd of more than 1,500 cheered wildly as the players celebrated on the ice. "That was a huge goal," says White, who had been selected the ECAC Player of the Year. "Kendice wasn't one of our main goal scorers, but that was the story of that team. Everyone contributed—a total team effort."

Cornell advanced to the NCAA Tournament, where they faced Harvard. The Crimson were no problem, even on their home ice, and the Big Red won 6–2. "That was almost surreal, beating Harvard like that," says White. "And we were so excited—here we are, going to the Frozen Four." A week later, the women faced Mercyhurst in the national semifinal at Ridder Arena in Minneapolis. The Lakers, ranked number 1 in the country, were undoubtedly confident after their two early-season victories over Cornell. But they quickly learned that they were facing a much tougher opponent this time.

Derraugh's team took the early lead on a shorthanded goal by

Sophomore Catherine White scored the first goal for Cornell in the ECAC championship game. An outstanding puck handler and goal scorer, she was named the ECAC Player of the Year for the 2009–10 season. (Patrick Shanahan/Cornell Athletic Communications)

Co-captain Liz Zorn played on a Big Red team that won only four games in her freshman year but went on to capture the ECAC championship when she was a senior. (Patrick Shanahan/Cornell Athletic Communications)

Cornell took a 3–0 lead, but Clarkson made a strong comeback in the third period, and when regulation time expired, the score was tied. A goal by Kendice Ogilvie (raising her arms) at 7:52 of overtime won the title for the Big Red. (Patrick Shanahan/Cornell Athletic Communications)

Ogilvie was mobbed by her teammates as the Lynah Faithful cheered. (Patrick Shanahan/Cornell Athletic Communications)

Fortino, who cashed in a rebound of a shot by Karlee Overguard '11. Mercyhurst evened the score midway through the second period; two minutes later, they tallied again to carry a 2–1 lead into the third period. The score was knotted again at 7:06 in the third, when Jess Martino '12 fired a pass across the crease to a wide-open Karlee Overguard. The score remained 2–2 as regulation time ended.

In the overtime, the Lakers pressed the attack, but Mazzotta refused to budge. She would make twenty-eight saves in the game. Then the Cornell women got a break: Amber Overguard '11 stole the puck in the offensive zone and fired a shot at Mercyhurst goalie Hillary Pattenden, who made the initial save but couldn't control the puck. "I was just off to the side of the net," says White, "and sure enough the puck came over to me. [Pattenden] was down, trying to protect the net, but her legs were open. I just pushed it through. The next thing I know, I'm on the bottom [of a pile of players]. There's hundreds of pounds on top of me, and I can't even breathe—but it doesn't matter."

Mercyhurst disputed the goal, claiming that the net was dislodged before the puck crossed the goal line, but a review upheld the result. The Big Red moved on to the national final.

The championship game was one of the most celebrated—and longest—contests in the history of women's hockey. Cornell faced Minnesota–Duluth, ranked number 2 and one of the most successful programs in the nation. Since the NCAA Tournament for women's hockey had been established in 2001, the Bulldogs had already played in five championship games, winning four. The two teams were evenly matched—and after regulation time expired, they were tied 2–2. They played one overtime period, then another, without a goal. In the third

ECAC commissioner Steve Hagwell presented the MVP trophy to Kendice Ogilvie. (Patrick Shanahan/Cornell Athletic Communications)

overtime, with only 33.6 seconds remaining, UMD's Jessica Wong finally broke through, ending the game and giving her team its fifth national title.

"That group of seniors, they had won four games their freshman year," says Mazzotta. "As underclassmen, we really wanted to win it for them. We were upset about losing, but Liz Zorn—one of the best captains I ever played for—was able to see the big picture. She was consoling us, and she was able to understand just how special that year really was." Mazzotta, who had made an NCAA-record sixty-one saves in the championship game, was named to the Frozen Four All-Tournament team along with teammates Fortino and Lauriane Rougeau '13.

❖ RENEWAL ON ICE ❖

After Bill Duthie's teams won six consecutive Ivy League women's hockey championships from 1976 to 1981—sharing the last one, reluctantly, with Brown—it would be nine years before Cornell would capture another Ivy title. The team led by Julie Andeberhan would win one more in 1996, but the ECAC championship, established in 1985, would prove elusive.

While the ECAC's membership has varied greatly over the years—more than thirty schools have belonged at one time or another—since 2006–07 it has had the same twelve members, and all twelve participate in both men's and women's ice hockey. These institutions include six Ivy League schools (all but Penn and Columbia) as well as Clarkson, Colgate, Quinnipiac, RPI, St. Lawrence, and Union.

Before the 2005–06 season, Doug Derraugh became the interim head coach of the women's team, and he set his sights on the ECAC title. The team had struggled to a 3–22–1 record in 2004–05 under head coach Melody Davidson, who departed after the season to coach the Canadian women's team in the 2006 Winter Olympics. Derraugh was asked to take over while she was gone. He had been an outstanding player for Cornell, scoring 153 points in 119 games and serving as co-captain in 1990–91. After graduating, he played professionally for thirteen years in Europe. Ready to move on with his career, he welcomed the opportunity to coach at his alma mater.

"I've always felt that Cornell should have a strong program," he says. "Where else can you go to get an Ivy League education in a beautiful place like Ithaca, New York? And then you combine that with the fact that ice hockey is, if not the number 1 sport, one of the top sports on campus. It's a great atmosphere."

In his first year, Derraugh's team posted an improving-but-not-there-yet record of 9–18–1. More important, he laid the groundwork as both a recruiter and behind-the-bench strategist for the team's ascendance. After the Winter Olympics, when Davidson accepted a full-time job with Hockey Canada, the word "interim" was dropped from Derraugh's title—and he set to work finding the players he needed to make his team

Doug Derraugh has coached the women's team since 2005, elevating the program to national prominence and winning four ECAC championships . . . so far. (Patrick Shanahan/Cornell Athletic Communications)

a top national program.

Derraugh did a good job convincing highly recruited skaters like Rebecca Johnston '12 to come to Cornell. "I had two older sisters who had played hockey, one at Cornell and the other at Harvard," says Johnston. "I went on visits to both schools, and Cornell seemed to suit me better. Doug Derraugh was really knowledgeable, I liked his coaching style, and I knew I'd learn a lot from him."

Johnston and other strong recruits such as Lauriane Rougeau, Catherine White, Laura Fortino, and Amanda Mazzotta were molded into a formidable unit under Derraugh's guidance. The team posted a 12–17–1 record in 2007–08 and was 12–14–5 the following year. For the 2009–10 season, Johnston took a year off from school to play on Canada's gold-medal Olympic team, but her Cornell teammates brought home the program's first ECAC title and nearly won the NCAA championship.

When Johnston returned for the 2010–11 season, the team was even stronger, winning another ECAC championship trophy and establishing a record for most wins in a season by any Cornell hockey team, men or women, with a 31–3–1 record. They were almost as dominating the following year, going 30–5, although they lost the ECAC championship game to St. Lawrence. "That was a memorable time," says Johnston. "How fast the program changed, how fast it turned around, to get to that next level and become one of the best in the country. It was pretty cool."

Coach Doug Derraugh (at right) joined his team for the customary team photo with the ECAC Tournament championship trophy. (Courtesy of Ned Dykes, Cornell Hockey Association)

In the 2010 ECAC Tournament final against Union, goalie Ben Scrivens would stop every shot he faced. He allowed only one goal in four conference playoff games that year. (Courtesy of George May)

A second-period goal by defenseman Sean Whitney gave Cornell a 2–0 lead. Ben Scrivens would do the rest. (Courtesy of Adriano Manocchia)

❋ ❋ ❋

The consistent play of an outstanding goalie was also the story for the men. All year, they had been getting superb efforts from Ben Scrivens, who posted four shutouts in the regular season—but he was just getting started. After finishing second to Yale by one point and earning a first-round bye, Cornell faced Harvard at Lynah in the best-of-three quarterfinals of the ECAC Tournament. The Big Red took the first game 5–1, which is notable because the opposition scored a goal (on a shot that bounced off a skate). It would be the last one that Scrivens would allow in the conference tournament.

On the next night, the Cornell men advanced by defeating Harvard 3–0. They traveled to Albany, where their semifinal opponent was Brown, a team with a losing record that had upset Yale in their quarterfinal series. Scrivens was once again impregnable, stopping twenty-three shots to record his eighteenth career shutout, tying David McKee's record. The final score was again 3–0.

The opponent in the ECAC championship game was Union, a talented young team that had defeated St. Lawrence 3–1 in their semifinal. They were good—but Scrivens was better. A penalty against the Dutchmen late in the first period put the Big Red on the power play, and Joe Devin '11 cashed in to put his team ahead 1–0. That score held up through most of the second period, but the result was still very much in doubt. "In any one-game elimination tournament like that," says defenseman Sean Whitney '12, "it just takes a fluke tying goal and then you're in overtime."

Late in the second, Union was called for too many men on the ice, putting Cornell's top power-play unit back in action. After a

The referee signals that Whitney's shot is a goal as the Cornell players begin to celebrate. (Courtesy of George May)

battle in the corner, Riley Nash sent the puck to the front of the net, where Whitney was waiting. "I was on the weak side," he says. "I thought I heard Schafe yelling, 'Whit, get to the net!' So I went there, and the puck just popped out [toward me]. I whacked it into the open net."

Whitney's quick shot beat Union netminder Keith Kinkaid by a split second, as the goalie extended his left leg to try to block the open net. It was the key moment, as a two-goal lead late in the game with Scrivens guarding the net was a formula for another Cornell victory. The final would once again be 3–0 after Patrick Kennedy '11 scored into an empty net in the final minute to secure the twelfth ECAC title for the men.

It was Scrivens's third straight shutout, moving him past

The Big Red were led by senior captain Colin Greening, who scored fifteen goals that season before moving on to a professional career with the NHL's Ottawa Senators. (Courtesy of George May)

Big Red assistant captain Riley Nash, like Colin Greening, would move on to an NHL career after leaving Cornell. (Courtesy of Adriano Manocchia)

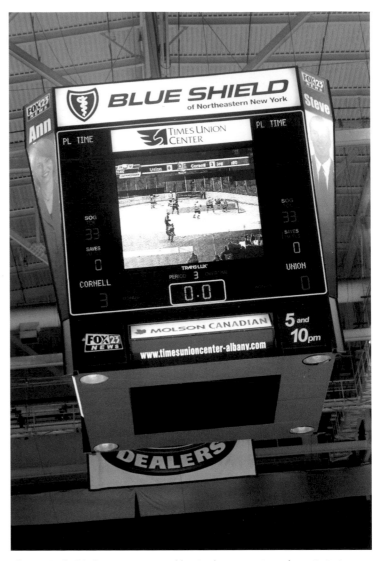

The Big Red added an empty-net goal late in the game to complete a 3–0 victory and secure their twelfth ECAC championship. (Courtesy of George May)

Ben Scrivens was named MVP of the tournament. He also won the Ken Dryden Award as the top ECAC goaltender that season and was selected a first-team All-American, the ninth Cornell goalie to be so honored. (Courtesy of George May)

As they left the ice, the Big Red players saluted the Lynah Faithful in Albany's Times Union Center. (Courtesy of George May)

David McKee as the Cornell career leader with nineteen. His scoreless streak stretched to 230 minutes and 34 seconds. He was named the winner of the Ken Dryden Award as the ECAC's top goaltender, a first-team All-American, and a Hobey Baker finalist. "I think they have the best goaltender in the country," said Union coach Nate Leaman after the game. "Scrivens is a huge difference maker back there."

Like the women, the men advanced to the NCAA Tournament. They had high hopes for a return to the Frozen Four, but ran into a powerhouse New Hampshire team in the first round and lost 6–2. While neither team got as far as they might have liked, they had made important contributions to what may have been the finest winter season in the history of Cornell athletics and were saluted at a campus celebration in April.

An excited group of Cornell players and coaches posed with the Whitelaw Cup after the game. (Courtesy of George May)

CORNELL 8, BOSTON UNIVERSITY 7 3OT
LYNAH RINK, ITHACA, NEW YORK, MARCH 10, 2012

It will always be remembered as the long weekend at Lynah.

On Friday night, the men defeated Dartmouth in the first of a best-of-three ECAC quarterfinal playoff series. The game went into a second overtime before Sean Whitney scored his first goal of the year to win it for Cornell 4–3. It had lasted 97 minutes and 40 seconds, making it the longest game ever played at Lynah Rink.

The next day, the women broke that record. Their game, an NCAA single-elimination contest for a trip to the Frozen Four, began at 2 p.m. The opponent was Boston University, the Hockey East champions and the team that had knocked them out of the

(facing page) Yes! Big Red players (left to right) Chelsea Karpenko, Jessica Campbell, and Kendice Ogilvie showed some emotion after completing—and winning—the longest hockey game in the history of Lynah Rink. (Courtesy of Ned Dykes, Cornell Hockey Association)

NCAA playoffs the previous year. BU jumped into the lead with two goals only thirty-four seconds apart early in the first period. Eleven minutes later, the Terriers added another tally. The Big Red got on the board late in the period, when Jessica Campbell '14 blocked a shot at the Cornell blue line and scored on a breakaway to make it 3–1.

During the period break, Doug Derraugh pulled senior goalie Amanda Mazzotta and inserted Lauren Slebodnick '14, with whom she had alternated during the season. Cornell captain Rebecca Johnston evened the score early in the second, getting a goal ten seconds into the period and tallying again three minutes later. BU coach Brian Durocher then called a time-out to calm his team, but it didn't do much good. Only forty-three seconds after play resumed, a one-timer by Laura Fortino put Cornell ahead. BU star Marie-Philip Poulin pulled her team even again at 15:01, but shortly after Brianne Jenner '15 took a feed from Johnston to

On March 10, 2012, Cornell faced Boston University at Lynah Rink in an NCAA quarterfinal playoff. As the teams lined up for the national anthems, none of the players suspected how long they would be on the ice that day. (Courtesy of Ned Dykes, Cornell Hockey Association)

BU jumped to an early 3–0 lead, but Jessica Campbell got her team on the board with a goal late in the first period. (Cornell Athletic Communications)

After the first period, Coach Doug Derraugh changed his goalie, inserting sophomore Lauren Slebodnick into the game to replace Amanda Mazzotta. (© Mark H. Anbinder, used by permission)

Cornell captain Rebecca Johnston scored twice early in the second period to tie the score at 3–3. She would add another goal in the third to complete her hat trick. (© Mark H. Anbinder, used by permission)

The Big Red continued to score. Cornell pulled ahead by one goal, then two, then three. By the middle of the third period, the home team led 7–4. (Courtesy of Ned Dykes, Cornell Hockey Association)

The Terriers battled back, scoring three power-play goals late in the third period to once again knot the score. It was 7–7 at the end of regulation time. (Courtesy of Ned Dykes, Cornell Hockey Association)

The tenor of the game changed abruptly in overtime, and it became a prolonged defensive battle. There was no scoring in the first overtime period—or the second. (Courtesy of Ned Dykes, Cornell Hockey Association)

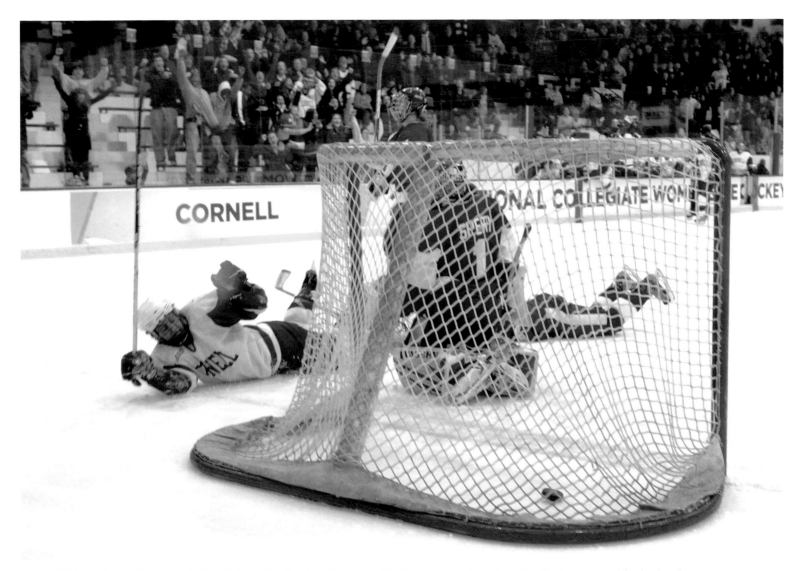

With less than a minute to go in the third overtime, Lauriane Rougeau grabbed a loose puck, broke into the offensive zone, and fired a shot that went between the legs of BU goalie Kerrin Sperry. (Courtesy of Ned Dykes, Cornell Hockcy Association)

Exhausted but elated, the rest of the Cornell players mobbed Rougeau.
(© Mark H. Anbinder, used by permission)

Leaping up, Jillian Saulnier celebrated the victory with the Lynah Faithful.
(Courtesy of Tanya Brennan)

tally the goal that made it 5–4 Cornell at the end of the second.

The scoring continued. Only eighteen seconds into the third, Johnston cashed in a turnover to put her team ahead 6–4. (A single hat floated down to the ice to salute her third goal of the game.) Six minutes later, Jenner knocked in a rebound for her second goal. Surely, a 7–4 lead in the third would be enough?

But it wasn't. Three penalties against Cornell, including a tripping call on Johnston with less than four minutes remaining, would lead to three BU power-play goals. The scoreboard read 7–7 as regulation time expired.

And then the scoring stopped. In the first overtime, BU goalie Kerrin Sperry turned aside fourteen Cornell shots while Slebodnick made nine saves. The second overtime was much the same, with the goalies dominating play. "It seemed like everything was going in the first three periods," said Derraugh after the game, "then both goalies were stopping everything in the overtime." The game went to a third extra period.

Five minutes went by, ten minutes, fifteen. Once again, the goalies (and the goalposts) were stopping everything. "During the first three periods, it just seemed like, *Oh they scored, no big deal. We can get one right back*," says Slebodnick. "But when we went to overtime, that didn't apply. It became more of a defensive game."

Cornell went on the power play twice but failed to score. BU crashed the offensive zone with an all-out rush but couldn't get a shot on net. The clock ticked down to the final minute of the period. And then Lauriane Rougeau snagged a loose puck. "I was in front of the net, trying to block shots," she says. "The puck was turned over close to our blue line, and I decided to just go for it. I didn't look at the clock, but I knew there wasn't a lot of time left. At that point, everyone was exhausted, so I just went up the ice and around a couple of players. I thought, *Why not try this move? I have nothing to lose.* I went around [the second defender] and was able to squeeze the puck between the goalie's legs." The red light went on with 10.1 seconds remaining.

Rougeau celebrated by using all the energy she had left to jump into the air, inciting the crowd into a wild celebration. She was soon buried beneath a pile of exhausted but elated teammates. The cheering of the Faithful rattled the walls of the old rink.

The game had gone on for 119 minutes and 50 seconds, shattering the record the men had set the night before. "I played here at Cornell, played thirteen years professionally, been coaching for seven years, and I don't think I've ever been involved in a game as crazy as that one," said Derraugh in the postgame press conference. "I don't think the fans will ever forget it."

The spectators who had showed up in midafternoon for the beginning of the marathon contest were augmented by the coaches and players for the men's team, whose game had to be pushed back forty-five minutes because the women were still playing when they arrived at Lynah. One benefit of the delay, recalls Sean Whitney, was "the electricity in the building" after the women's victory. The Big Red men were clearly energized by the buzz, scoring three goals in the first period, including another by Whitney, to defeat Dartmouth 3–1 and advance to the ECAC semifinal. While both teams would lose in the next round of the playoffs, that weekend they had left their mark in the storied history of Lynah Rink.

Cornell goalies Lauren Slebodnick (left) and Amanda Mazzotta had big smiles after their team's historic victory. (Courtesy of Ned Dykes, Cornell Hockey Association)

The victorious Big Red players raised their sticks to salute the Lynah Faithful, who had just witnessed the longest game in the history of the rink. (Courtesy of Ned Dykes, Cornell Hockey Association)

CORNELL 5, MICHIGAN 1
MADISON SQUARE GARDEN, NEW YORK CITY, NOVEMBER 24, 2012

It was billed as the Frozen Apple, but it might have been called the Clash of the Titans: the Big Red battling the University of Michigan, one of the most storied college hockey programs in the nation, winners of nine NCAA championships, at Madison Square Garden. The Wolverines were led by the legendary Red Berenson, in his twenty-eighth year as the head coach.

The historic arena was once again packed on the Saturday night after Thanksgiving, and the Big Red quickly jumped ahead on a first-period power-play goal by Joel Lowry '15. The lead stretched to 3–0 in the second, as Teemu Tiitinen '16 scored his

first career goal and Greg Miller '13 beat Wolverine goalie Steve Racine three minutes later. "It was a great setup by Brian Ferlin '15 and Joel Lowry, my linemates," says Miller. "I didn't have to do much but tap it in backdoor."

During the second period, the Cornell players wore special gray-and-white camouflage jerseys to honor the Wounded Warrior Project. The jerseys were later auctioned, with the proceeds going to the charity service organization. "It's just a great organization to support," said head coach Mike Schafer. "We have [center] Cole Bardreau '15, his brother's in the military, and [equipment manager] Sean Schmidt, his brother's in the military, so there's some connection with our players and staff. It's a great opportunity for us to raise awareness."

In the previous season, Cornell and Michigan had squared off in the NCAA Midwest Regional at the Resch Center in Green Bay, Wisconsin, with the Big Red taking a thrilling 3–2

(*facing page*) The success of the first Red Hot Hockey game at Madison Square Garden in 2007 led to more college games in "The World's Most Famous Arena," including a 2012 matchup between Cornell and the University of Michigan. (Courtesy of Ned Dykes, Cornell Hockey Association)

In the Frozen Apple at Madison Square Garden, Cornell faced the University of Michigan. Once again, the arena was filled, although this time it was easier to tell the fans apart, as the Wolverine rooters were wearing blue and maize. (Courtesy of Ned Dykes, Cornell Hockey Association)

overtime victory. Both teams had started the 2012–13 season somewhat unevenly—Cornell was 3-3-2 and Michigan 5-6-1—but that didn't diminish the excitement about the Frozen Apple. Blue-and-maize clad Wolverine fans and the Faithful in their familiar red-and-white outfits filled every seat.

"It can be a tad overwhelming to play there," says Greg Miller, who had faced BU in two previous games at MSG. "Schafe always preached that: to enjoy the moment but remember we're there for a job, too. But, boy, when you hear that roar after you score a goal, it's like nothing else. The sound of the crowd, of the 18,000-plus. So loud! And there are certain characteristics of Cornell fans—you're able to relate to them, and it gives you that 'home' sort of feeling, like when you're at Lynah."

In the third period, Cornell tri-captain Erik Axell '13 made it 4–0 before Michigan got on the board at 9:24. Goalie Andy Iles '14 was disappointed to lose the shutout, but he remained focused and stopped every Wolverine shot after that, finishing the game with twenty-seven saves. As the last few minutes ticked away on the big video display, Miller completed the scoring with his second tally of the night to make the final score 5–1.

"It really doesn't ever get old, and the crowd was absolutely phenomenal," said Mike Schafer after the game. "There's a special bond at Cornell between the hockey program, its alumni, its faculty and its townspeople, and there is not a greater place to put it on display than Madison Square Garden."

The victory appeared to energize the Big Red, and they won their next three games in a row. It was up and down after that, and their season ended in an ECAC quarterfinal series at

Quinnipiac. For the players on that team, though, the victory over Michigan was an enduring highlight of their time at Cornell. "It really was more than just a game," says Iles. "We thrived on that atmosphere, thrived on the opportunity to wear the Cornell jersey in front of so many alumni and so many supporters. It was all about your university, all about Cornell pride. The stadium was packed with Cornell fans who were invested in us. It was an amazing experience."

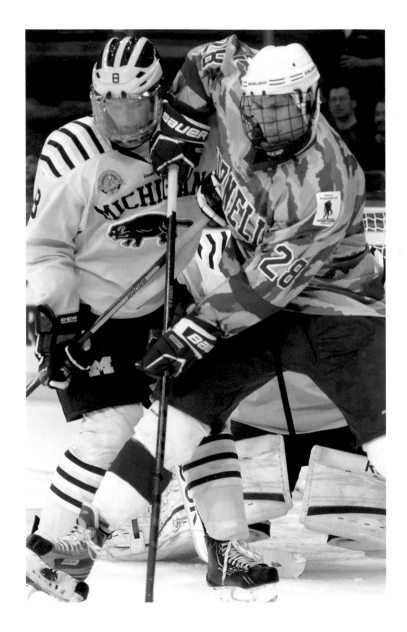

Cornell took the lead on a first-period power-play goal by hardworking forward Joel Lowry. (Courtesy of Ned Dykes, Cornell Hockey Association)

In the second period, the Big Red players wore special camouflage jerseys to honor the Wounded Warrior Project, as seen in this photo of Dustin Mowrey. The jerseys were later auctioned, with the funds going to the service charity. (Courtesy of Ned Dykes, Cornell Hockey Association)

Cornell increased its lead to 2–0 on the first career goal by freshman forward Teemu Tiitinen (19), who slipped the puck past Michigan goalie Steve Racine. (Courtesy of Ned Dykes, Cornell Hockey Association)

With Cornell holding a 1–0 lead, the sellout crowd focused intently on the action early in the second period. (Courtesy of Michigan Photography)

The Wolverines were back on their heels for much of the second period, and Greg Miller pushed the Cornell lead to 3–0 with a tap-in goal. "It was a great setup by Brian Ferlin and Joel Lowry, my linemates," he says. Miller would score again in the third. (Patrick Shanahan/Cornell Athletic Communications)

The game was feisty at times, as seen in this confrontation between 6-foot-5 forward Armand de Swardt and a group of Michigan players. Order was maintained by the officials. (Courtesy of Ned Dykes, Cornell Hockey Association)

Junior goalie Andy Iles was outstanding, frustrating many Wolverine scoring attempts on his way to twenty-seven saves. (Courtesy of Ned Dykes, Cornell Hockey Association)

Shortly after winning this faceoff against Michigan's A. J. Treais, tri-captain Erik Axell made it 4–0 in favor of the Big Red in the third period. (Patrick Shanahan/ Cornell Athletic Communications)

The Big Red saluted the Lynah Faithful before leaving the ice. After the game, Mike Schafer praised the "special bond" between the Cornell team and its supporters saying, "There is not a greater place to put it on display than Madison Square Garden." (Courtesy of Ned Dykes, Cornell Hockey Association)

CORNELL 2, HARVARD 1
LYNAH RINK, ITHACA, NEW YORK, MARCH 10, 2013

Cornell 1, Harvard 1. Lynah Rink packed with the Faithful. Two minutes remaining in the game and an ECAC championship on the line.

In 2012–13, the Big Red women had won their fourth consecutive ECAC regular-season title and had an impressive 23–5–1 record as they moved on to the conference playoffs. In the quarterfinals, they bested Colgate in two nail-biters, winning the first 5–4 in overtime and taking the second 3–2 by scoring twice in the last minute. The game winner, tallied by Brianne Jenner, came with 00:01 on the clock. Somehow, they had managed to win both games while leading for only one second.

(facing page) The championship game of the 2013 ECAC Tournament was a hard-fought, close-checking contest between two longtime rivals. Here, a pair of Harvard defenders tries to prevent Jessica Campbell from getting to the net. (Courtesy of Patrick Shanahan/Cornell Athletic Communications)

In the semifinal, freshman forward Taylor Woods '16 put on a show, scoring a hat trick to lead the Big Red over St. Lawrence 4–2. Once again, it was on to the championship game against their rival from Cambridge. The teams were evenly matched and had split their two regular-season games, each winning on their home rink. Almost 2,500 fans were packed into Lynah for the championship contest, and the vocal support of the Faithful was deafening as the game began.

The Big Red came out fast, outshooting the Crimson fourteen to seven in the first period and getting a goal from Jenner to take the lead. Before the game, Doug Derraugh had praised his star forward, the Ivy League Player of the Year. "[Jenner] can do everything," he said. "She does everything at such a high level. From her vision on the ice, to her fast hands, to her power, she can beat you in so many ways."

Harvard evened the score late in the first period on a hard

(top) Almost 2,500 fans packed into Lynah Rink to see the 2013 ECAC championship game between Cornell and Harvard. One of them held a sign that proved to be prophetic. (Courtesy of Ned Dykes, Cornell Hockey Association)

(right) As the teams lined up for the pregame ceremony, the Big Red players were hoping to add one more banner to the array in the rafters. (Courtesy of Ned Dykes, Cornell Hockey Association)

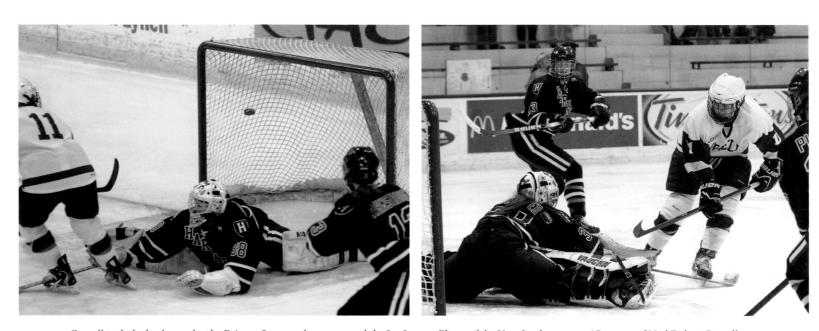

Cornell took the lead on a shot by Brianne Jenner, who was named the Ivy League Player of the Year for that season. (Courtesy of Ned Dykes, Cornell Hockey Association [*left*], and Patrick Shanahan/Cornell Athletic Communications [*right*])

Harvard tied the score in the first period on a shot that bounced off junior goalie Lauren Slebodnick's blocker and flipped into the net. It would prove to be their only cause for celebration that day. (Courtesy of Ned Dykes, Cornell Hockey Association)

Teammates Hayleigh Cudmore (24) and Jillian Saulnier (19) were the first to congratulate Jenner after her goal. (Courtesy of Ned Dykes, Cornell Hockey Association)

After allowing Harvard's first-period goal, Lauren Slebodnick was perfect the rest of the way, turning away all scoring attempts and making eighteen saves in the game. (Photo courtesy of Ned Dykes, Cornell Hockey Association)

A Harvard penalty late in the game gave the Big Red a great opportunity—and Jessica Campbell cashed it in, snaring a rebound and knocking it into the goal for the game winner. (Patrick Shanahan/Cornell Athletic Communications)

shot by Hillary Crowe that hit goalie Lauren Slebodnick's blocker and then flipped over her head and into the goal. Then the defense took over. In the second, Cornell allowed only a single shot on Slebodnick (and one that hit the post) while launching ten that were stopped by Harvard goalie Emerance Maschmeyer. The score remained 1–1.

Both teams had power-play opportunities in the third, but it was Cornell's second advantage that proved crucial. Harvard's Sarah Edney was sent off for slashing at 16:32, and the Big Red pushed the puck ahead, into the right corner of the offensive zone. After a battle for possession, Jessica Campbell passed the puck to Emily Fulton '15 in front of the net. "She kind of made a nice move and deked out the goalie," said Campbell after the game. "[The puck] popped out and somehow literally landed on my stick. I had a completely open net." With 1:40 left, Campbell's goal moved Cornell ahead 2–1.

Harvard coach Katey Stone pulled Maschmeyer for one last push, but the Crimson's extra-attacker offense came up empty. The buzzer sounded, the Big Red women hoisted the championship trophy for the third time in four years, and the Lynah Faithful celebrated.

"I don't think you can say enough about the crowd," said defenseman Alyssa Gagliardi '14 after the postgame celebration. "The support that we got from other students and the community was incredible. It's like your sixth man out there. It definitely helps a lot, and we couldn't thank everyone enough for coming out."

In the NCAA Tournament, another rival was waiting: Mercyhurst. The game, played before a raucous crowd at Lynah, was a

As the final buzzer sounded, the Cornell players rushed off the bench to begin their championship celebration. (Patrick Shanahan/Cornell Athletic Communications)

Assistant captain Laura Fortino enjoyed the moment, displaying the championship trophy to the Lynah Faithful. (Patrick Shanahan/ Cornell Athletic Communications)

Athletic director Andy Noel (far left) joined the smiling coaches and players on the ice as the Big Red women celebrated their third ECAC Tournament championship in four years. They would add another in 2014. (Courtesy of Ned Dykes, Cornell Hockey Association)

hard-fought affair—fifteen penalties were called—that found the Big Red down by a goal, 3–2, with less than a minute to go. Derraugh pulled Slebodnick, and Cornell got an offensive-zone faceoff after Mercyhurst was called for icing. Brianne Jenner won the draw and got the puck to forward Jillian Saulnier '15, whose slap shot beat Mercyhurst goalie Stephanie Ciampa to knot the score with 55.6 seconds remaining. Neither team scored in the remaining time, sending the contest to overtime. Unlike the previous year's battle with BU, this one was resolved quickly, with Mercyhurst's Jenna Dingeldein knocking in a rebound at 4:49 to end it.

✦ ✦ ✦

The following year, the Big Red women won another ECAC Tournament title, defeating Clarkson (who would go on to win the NCAA championship) 1–0 at Cheel Arena in Potsdam, New York. The victory was one more sterling accomplishment for Doug Derraugh's team. After going 21–9–6 and securing their first ECAC title in 2010, they had followed that with records of 31–3–1, 30–5–0, 27–6–1, and 24–6–4. Over those five seasons, they set a new standard for most wins by a Cornell hockey team, won the ECAC championship four times, and advanced to the NCAA Tournament each year—adding an array of new banners to the Lynah rafters and another outstanding chapter to the ongoing story of Cornell hockey.

EPILOGUE

AS MIKE SCHAFER SAID AFTER THE VICTORY over Michigan at Madison Square Garden in 2012, there is a "special bond" between Cornell's hockey teams and the Lynah Faithful. It extends beyond students and alumni to encompass faculty, staff, townies, parents, friends, and almost anyone else who has been to a game at Lynah Rink or any of the out-of-town venues where Big Red fans gather to support the teams. As Faithful stalwart Steve Worona '70 once put it, "Cornell isn't an organization. It's a loose affiliation of independent fiefdoms united by a common hockey team." His tongue may have been in cheek, but the sentiment rings true. Nothing brings Cornellians together like a hockey game.

Seeing the action at Lynah can make a lasting impression on anyone—especially young recruits. "You can tell them about it,"

(*facing page*) The strong connection between Cornell's players and the Lynah Faithful forges lifelong memories for everyone involved in the Cornell hockey program. (Courtesy of Ned Dykes, Cornell Hockey Association)

says Topher Scott, Cornell's co-captain in 2007–08 and an assistant coach from 2011 to 2016, "but when they experience it, it's really special. They sit across from the student section, and they're able to see and hear all the cheers and chants. They're usually pretty wide-eyed after the game. It's definitely an advantage in the recruiting process."

Goalie Mitch Gillam '17, who was recruited by Scott, confirms the impact. "My first time at Lynah was pretty cool," he says. "I remember sitting there and thinking that it was one of the best atmospheres I'd ever seen. I couldn't imagine playing in a better place, so when I got the call from Topher that they wanted me to come, it was a no-brainer."

When recruits become team members, the backing of the Faithful becomes a vital part of their Cornell experience. And it stays with them—even years later, they can recall how it energized and inspired them at key moments. Looking back at the NCAA championship game that capped the undefeated season of the 1969–70 men's team, Garth Ryan told me, "One of my most vivid memories is the fans. Overwhelming. I remember that clearly, the tremendous support."

The memories are vivid for the Faithful, too—sit down with Cornell hockey fans and ask them about their favorite moments, and you're going to be there for a while, whether they saw their first game in 1962 or 1992 or last week. For me, it was in the fall of 1967. That spring, a few months before I moved into U-Hall 5 on West Campus, Cornell had won its first NCAA championship—so I figured we had a good team. I made my way up the hill to Lynah Rink and found a spot on the benches.

I think the opponent was RPI. There was a big guy named Dryden in goal, and he was something, stopping almost every shot that came his way and standing there, leaning on his stick, to watch the action at the other end when his teammates were on the attack. Which was most of the time.

Cornell won the game, and I was hooked. I kept going to Lynah, because the Big Red didn't disappoint—and they didn't lose. Their sixty-three-game home winning streak began before I arrived and ended after I graduated. They didn't lose many games away from Lynah, either, and I remember traveling to Boston Garden to watch them win the ECAC playoffs and listening on the radio as the 1969–70 team completed its undefeated season to secure another national championship.

Ultimately, being a member of the Lynah Faithful goes beyond goals and saves, beyond wins and losses. It's the intensity of the shared experience and the feeling that you're part of a tradition that has meant so much to so many, on the ice and in the stands. "Every game is awesome with that crowd," says Gillam, "and there's such a rich history." He concludes:

"KEN DRYDEN STOOD IN THE SAME CREASE WHERE I'M PLAYING. THAT'S PRETTY DAMN COOL."

Big Red goalie Mitch Gillam was proud to play in the same crease where Ken Dryden had guarded the net at Lynah Rink fifty years before. (Courtesy of Ned Dykes, Cornell Hockey Association)

WHAT'S DAVE WEARING?

For the Lynah Faithful, one of the great moments at every home game is seeing Dave Nulle's outfit when he rolls out to groom the ice. Over the years, his costumes have become more and more elaborate and entertaining, whether he's channeling Elvis or George Washington or Ramses the Great—or honoring the Big Red marching band.

(All photos © Mark H. Anbinder, used by permission)

(Courtesy of Adriano Manocchia)

THE STATISTICS

THE ESSENTIAL WOMEN'S NUMBERS

A full set of statistics is available on the "History" page of the Cornell women's hockey website, http://www.cornellbigred.com/index.aspx?path=whockey.

CHAMPIONSHIPS

Ivy League	ECAC Tournament
1976	2010
1977	2011
1978	2013
1979	2014
1980	
1981*	
1990	
1996	
2010	
2011	
2012	
2013*	
2017	

* Shared title

COACHING HISTORY

Coach	Years	Record	Winning pct.
Bill Duthie	1972–84	135–85–5	.611
Dave Harackiewicz	1984–89	53–52–9	.504
Keith Howie	1989–90	14–4–0	.778
Dorothy Diggs	1990–93	19–31–4	.389
Julie Andeberhan	1993–98	53–61–6	.467
Carol Mullins	1998–02	47–66–3	.418
Melody Davidson	2002–05	14–64–7	.206
Doug Derraugh*	2005–17	222–135–33	.612

* Active as of date of publication

MOST CAREER GOALS

Player	Goals	Seasons
Cheryl Hines	155	1976–80
Digit Degidio	123	1979–83
Rebecca Johnston	97	2007–09, 2010–12
Cyndy Schlaepfer	95	1975–78
Brianne Jenner	93	2010–13, 2014–15
Cindy Warren	87	1977–81
Amy Stanzin	84	1982–86
Jillian Saulnier	80	2011–15
Sunshine Lorenz	75	1974–78
Chelsea Karpenko	68	2008–12

MOST CAREER ASSISTS

Player	Assists	Seasons
Brianne Jenner	136	2010–13, 2014–15
Cindy Warren	130	1977–81
Cheryl Hines	125	1976–80
Jillian Saulnier	114	2011–15
Cyndy Schlaepfer	104	1975–78
Catherine White	101	2008–12
Laura Fortino	98	2009–13
Rebecca Johnston	91	2007–09, 2010–12
Digit Degidio	90	1979–83
Lauriane Rougeau	89	2009–13

MOST CAREER POINTS

Player	Points	Seasons
Cheryl Hines	280	1976–80
Brianne Jenner	229	2010–13, 2014–15
Cindy Warren	217	1977–81
Digit Degidio	213	1979–83
Cyndy Schlaepfer	199	1975–78
Jillian Saulnier	194	2011–15
Rebecca Johnston	188	2007–09, 2010–12
Catherine White	167	2008–12
Amy Stanzin	157	1982–86
Diane Dillon	144	1979–83

CAREER GOALTENDING

Player	GAA	Seasons
Amanda Mazzotta	1.53	2008–12
Lauren Slebodnick	1.65	2010–14
Paula Voorheis	2.14	2013–17
Melissa Junkala	2.20	1995–99
Alanna Hayes	2.60	1995–99
Kayla Strong	2.68	2007–09
Laura MacPhail	2.82	1977–79
Jennie Niesluchowski	3.12	2006–09
Kathryn LoPresti	3.15	1985–89
Sanya Sandahl	3.21	1999–03

Note: Sorted by goals-against average; minimum 900 minutes

THE ESSENTIAL MEN'S NUMBERS

A full set of statistics is available on the "History" page of the Cornell men's hockey website, http://www.cornellbigred.com/index.aspx?path=mhockey.

CHAMPIONSHIPS

Ivy League		ECAC Tournament	NCAA Tournament
1966	1984*	1967	1967
1967	1985*	1968	1970
1968	1996	1969	
1969	1997	1970	
1970	2002	1973	
1971	2003	1980	
1972	2004*	1986	
1973	2005	1996	
1977	2012	1997	
1978	2014	2003	
1983*		2005	
		2010	

* Shared title

COACHING HISTORY

Coach	Years	Record	Winning pct.
G. A. Smith	1900–01	3–0–0	1.000
Talbot Hunter	1909–12, 1914–16	18–15–0	.545
Edmund Magner	1912–13	0–7–0	.000
E. J. Sawyer	1913–14	1–4–0	.200
Nicholas Bawlf	1920–47	45–76–4	.376
Arthur Boeringer	1947–48	0–4–0	.000
Paul Patten	1957–63	38–68–3	.362
Ned Harkness	1963–70	163–27–2	.854
Dick Bertrand	1970–82	230–103–9	.686
Lou Reycroft	1982–87	74–58–9	.557
Brian McCutcheon	1987–95	108–105–21	.506
Mike Schafer*	1995–17	412–242–89	.614

* Active as of date of publication

MOST CAREER GOALS

Player	Goals	Seasons
Brock Tredway	113	1977–81
Roy Kerling	93	1977–82
Doug Ferguson	91	1964–67
Lance Nethery	91	1975–79
Duanne Moeser	81	1982–86
Joe Nieuwendyk	73	1984–87
Jim Vaughan	71	1974–77
Matt Moulson	71	2002–06
John Hughes	68	1967–70
Pete Tufford	68	1966–69
Trent Andison	68	1987–91

MOST CAREER ASSISTS

Player	Assists	Seasons
Lance Nethery	180	1975–79
Larry Fullan	108	1969–72
Roy Kerling	107	1977–82
Gary Cullen	105	1981–85
Doug Ferguson	96	1964–67
Duanne Moeser	96	1982–86
Brian Cornell	95	1966–69
Brock Tredway	94	1977–81
Brian Campbell	92	1973–76
Pete Tufford	92	1966–69

MOST CAREER POINTS

Player	Points	Seasons
Lance Nethery	271	1975–79
Brock Tredway	207	1977–81
Roy Kerling	200	1977–82
Doug Ferguson	187	1964–67
Duanne Moeser	177	1982–86
Larry Fullan	165	1969–72
Pete Tufford	160	1966–69
Gary Cullen	159	1981–85
Jim Vaughan	154	1974–77
Doug Derraugh	153	1987–91

CAREER GOALTENDING

Player	Seasons	Gms	Min	GA	Saves	Save%	SO	Record	GAA
David LeNeveu	2001–03	46	2,788	60	914	.938	11	39–5–2	1.29
Ken Dryden	1966–69	83	4,844	128	1,987	.939	13	76–4–1	1.59
David McKee	2003–06	102	6,193	177	2,208	.926	18	65–24–13	1.74
Ben Scrivens	2006–10	117	6,710	216	2,873	.930	19	65–37–13	1.93
Brian Cropper	1968–71	59	3,325	117	1,347	.920	7	50–5–0	2.11
Mitch Gillam	2013–17	97	5,577	200	2,403	.923	11	47–28–17	2.15
Andy Iles	2010–14	118	7,140	269	2,988	.917	9	57–41–17	2.26
Troy Davenport	2004–05 2006–09	30	1,493	57	525	.902	2	11–9–2	2.29
Dave Quarrie	1964–67	19	963	37	324	.900	2	11–5–0	2.31
Matt Underhill	1998–02	89	5,070	196	2,052	.913	6	42–32–9	2.32

Note: Sorted by goals-against average; minimum 900 minutes

NOTE FROM THE AUTHOR

After I was hired in 2000 as the editor and publisher of *Cornell Alumni Magazine*, I wrote a column to explain my editorial philosophy. I noted that one of my predecessors, John Marcham '50, believed strongly in accurate, unbiased coverage of the university, and I stated that "I intend to adhere as closely as possible to Marcham's position of 'sympathetic objectivity' when reporting on all things Cornell—with the possible exception of the hockey team, about which I am hopelessly biased."

True. I was a dedicated member of the Lynah Faithful as a student, and I tried to follow Cornell hockey as best I could, in those pre-Internet days, between my graduation and my return to Ithaca almost thirty years later. Shortly after I got back, I secured a pair of men's hockey season tickets. (Don't ask.) It was a kick to go back to Lynah, which looked much the same—although now there were a lot of banners hanging from the rafters. The experience of being a member of the Faithful had lost none of its luster.

And there was a very good women's team, too, making it possible to spend even more time on those cold, hard benches.

So, needless to say, it was exciting when I was contacted by Jonathan Hall of Cornell University Press. He knew I had covered hockey in *CAM* and wondered if I might be interested in writing a book about Cornell hockey. Are you kidding?

The process of researching and writing this book has been a great pleasure. I've learned a lot about hockey and a lot about what makes Cornell's hockey program so special. I have a great many people to thank for making that possible.

First, and most important, this book would not have been possible without my classmate Arthur Mintz. He has been the voice of Lynah Rink since 1987 and knows the program inside and out. He helped me select the featured games, provided information about resources, sent me dozens of newspaper articles, reviewed thousands of photographs, answered questions, checked facts, made corrections, offered critiques, and was an invaluable research partner in many other ways. As the Faithful say when Arthur announces that there's one minute remaining in the period, "Thank you!"

I was pleased when Ken Dryden responded quickly to my inquiry about writing a foreword—and even more pleased when he said yes. Ken is as modest as he is brilliant, and it was an honor to work with him. He also gave me some great insights into the Cornell teams that he played on and the 1967 NCAA championship game.

My research into the featured games focused on newspaper accounts (most of them in the *Cornell Daily Sun* and the *Ithaca Journal*), box scores, press releases, and interviews with participants. I am greatly indebted to all the Big Red players and coaches I spoke with for their help (and their patience): Dick Bertrand, Brad Chartrand, Charlie Cook, Matt Cooney, Brian Cropper, Jim Crozier, Murray Deathe, Margaret Degidio (Digit Murphy), Doug Derraugh, Diane Dillon, Bill Duthie, Dave Elenbaas, Darren Eliot, Mitch Gillam, Chris Grenier, Karl Habib, Alanna Hayes (Burt), John Hughes, Andy Iles, Rebecca Johnston, Casey Jones, Laing Kennedy, Kyle Knopp, Ross Lemon, Dan Lodboa, Sunshine Lorenz (Diana Lorenz Weggler), Kent Manderville, Rudy Mateka, Amanda Mazzotta, Brian McCutcheon, Bob McGuinn, David McKee, Mark McRae, Matt McRae, Greg Miller, Matt Moulson, Lance Nethery, Joe Nieuwendyk, Sam Paolini, Lou Reycroft, Lauriane Rougeau, Garth Ryan, Mike Sancimino, Mike Schafer, Cyndy Schlaepfer (Youker), Topher Scott, Lauren Slebodnick, Marty Tormey, Brock Tredway, Pete Tufford, Ryan Vesce, Catherine White, Sean Whitney, and Steve Wilson.

Because of this book's focus on selected games, some of the most important players in Cornell hockey history are mentioned only in passing or not at all. I apologize to all the great players who were left out, and I urge every reader to peruse the statistics and search out other accounts of Cornell hockey to get the complete picture. It's a big story—too big for one book.

Special thanks to Roy Ives, who called Cornell hockey games on the radio for almost twenty years, for sharing his memories with me. A tip of the hat to a number of others who answered questions and provided research assistance, including Larry Baum '72, Sue Detzer, Diane Duthie '75, Ned Dykes '74, Corey Earle '07, Evan Earle '02, Lowell Frank '99, John Gaines '67, Ken Gilstein '70, Bill Howard '74, Laura Linke '73, and Scott Pesner '87. And also to the many contributors to elynah.com for providing so much information (and some invigorating commentary) on Big Red hockey and its many quirks and traditions.

I wrote about hockey and edited hockey articles written by others throughout my fourteen years at *CAM*. I adapted material from some of my stories for this book and also used information from other articles, including several by Brad Herzog '90, a superb writer and member in good standing of the Lynah Faithful (even though he lives in California). And I am grateful to the late Art Kaminsky '68; working with him on his 2002 *CAM* article about Ned Harkness was a crucial part of my education about hockey.

Two books were especially helpful as I researched Cornell's hockey history: *Good Sports: A History of Cornell Athletics* by Robert J. Kane (Cornell University, 1992) and *Cornell University Hockey* by Adam Wodon with research by Arthur Mintz (Arcadia, 2004).

Jeremy Hartigan and his colleagues in Cornell Athletic Communications, Brandon Thomas, Amanda Nicole Ghysel, John Lukach, and Julie Greco, provided valuable support and unearthed important material in their files. The cornellbigred.com website and my well-thumbed copy of the 2008–09 men's hockey media guide were key sources of information. I'm also indebted to Brian Kelley, assistant athletic director for communications at Boston University, who put me in touch with Jack Parker, the former BU player and coach who gave me a wonderful perspective on the Cornell-BU rivalry from the other side of the rink. (And I will note that Brian, an Ithaca College alumnus, worked at Cornell for four years before going to BU. So he knows something about the Lynah Faithful.)

At the *Cornell Daily Sun*, John Schroeder, Amy Wilson, and Reuben Arce provided valuable assistance in our photo research.

Many others provided photos or helped us to locate them, shared memories, offered suggestions, or just helped to move this project along in some way. The list is long, and I apologize in advance to anyone whose name I have omitted: Neil Ament, Mark Anbinder, Melissa Bauman, Mark Bedics, Howard Borkan, Norman Boucher, Tanya Brennan, Dave Bridgeman, Craig Campbell, Paul Capobianco, Tabitha Cary, Don Danila, Louise Vacca Dawe, Ron Demer, Dan Duffy, Ned Dykes, Marcie Farwell, Gene German, Aaron Griffin, Dale Grossman, Richard Hoffman, Robert Hoffmeister, Amy Andersen Kelsey, Edward Krajewski, Florence Labelle, Melanie Lefkowitz, Brock Malone, Adriano Manocchia, Rudy Mateka, George May, Gary Mikel, Elizabeth Muller, Gene Nighman, Carol Worman Nolan, David Null, Eric Peterson, Lisa Sergi, Jim Sherrill, Dale Steenberg, Susan Stein, Roberta Bandel Walcer, Jeffrey Weinstein, Joe Wilensky, Adam Wodon,

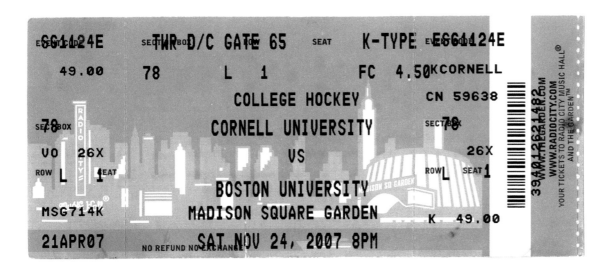

My ticket from the first Red Hot Hockey game at Madison Square Garden, which I attended with my family. We were all wearing red.

David Wohlhueter, and Hilary Dorsch Wong—along with a number of photographers not named here whose collections were perused for possible usage.

Michael McGandy, my editor at Cornell University Press, gave me excellent guidance throughout the writing and editing process, helping to shape my manuscript into this book. He also devoted many days to locating, identifying, and preparing the photographs that appear on these pages. Thanks also to Susan Specter (production editor) and Scott Levine (designer), as well as Jonathan Hall, Jennifer Longley, Diana Silva, and Bethany Wasik. Even with all this expert help, I suspect some errors and omissions remain, for which I take full responsibility.

Finally, many thanks to my wife, Susan, who now comments on good plays and bad calls in hockey games, looks at me, and says, "It's all your fault." And to our son, Miles, and daughter, Nadia, who both did their time on the benches at Lynah Rink with me. My family has been great about tolerating my lengthy hockey-related monologues as I worked on this book. And I will not mention that my wife and son are alumni of a certain university, so they root for the wrong team at Red Hot Hockey games.

INDEX

Page numbers in *italics* indicate photographs.